JOURNAL

OF THE

CONSTITUTIONAL CONVENTION

OF THE

DISTRICT OF MAINE:

WITH THE

ARTICLES OF SEPARATION,

AND

GOVERNOR BROOKS' PROCLAMATION,

PREFIXED.

1819-20.

Augusta:
FULLER & FULLER, PRINTERS TO THE STATE.
1856.

ARTICLES OF SEPARATION.

COMMONWEALTH OF MASSACHUSETTS.

An Act relating to the separation of the District of Maine from Massachusetts proper, and forming the same into a separate and independent State.

Whereas, It has been represented to this Legislature, that a majority of the people of the District of Maine are desirous of establishing a separate and independent Government within said District; Therefore,

SECTION 1. *Be it enacted by the Senate and House of Representatives, in General Court assembled, and by the authority of the same,* That the consent of this Commonwealth be, and the same is hereby given, that the District of Maine may be formed and erected into a separate and independent State, if the people of the said District shall, in the manner, and by the majority, hereinafter mentioned, express their consent and agreement thereto, upon the following terms and conditions; *and, provided,* the Congress of the United States shall give its consent thereto, before the fourth day of March next; which terms and conditions are as follows, viz:

First. All the lands and buildings belonging to the Commonwealth, within Massachusetts proper, shall continue to belong to said Commonwealth; and all the lands belonging to the Commonwealth, within the District of Maine, shall belong, the one-half thereof, to the said Commonwealth, and the other half thereof, to the State to be formed within the said District, to be divided as is hereinafter mentioned; and the lands within the said District which shall belong to the said Commonwealth, shall be free from taxation, while the title to the said lands remains in the Commonwealth; and the rights of the Commonwealth to their lands, within said District, and the remedies for the recovery thereof, shall continue the same within the proposed State, and in the courts thereof, as they now are within the said Commonwealth, and in the courts thereof; for which purposes, and for the maintenance of its rights, and recovery of its lands, the said Commonwealth shall be entitled to all other proper and legal remedies, and may appear in the courts of the proposed State, and in the courts of the United States, holden therein, and prosecute as a party, under the name and style of the Commonwealth of Massachusetts; and all rights of action for, or entry into lands, and of actions upon bonds, for the breach of the performance of the condition of settling duties, so called, which have accrued, or may accrue, shall remain in this Commonwealth, to be enforced, commuted, released, or otherwise disposed of, in such manner as this Commonwealth may hereafter determine; *provided, however,* that whatever this Commonwealth may hereafter receive or obtain on account thereof, if anything, shall, after deducting all reasonable charges relating thereto, be divided, one-third part thereof, to the new State, and two-third parts thereof, to this Commonwealth.

Second. All the arms which have been received by this Commonwealth from the United States, under the law of Congress, entitled " An act making provision for arming and equipping the whole body of Militia of the United States," passed April the twenty-third, one thousand eight hundred and eight, shall, as soon as the said District shall become a separate State, be divided between the two States, in proportion to the returns of the militia, according to which, the said arms have been received from the United States, as aforesaid.

Third. All moneys, stock, or other proceeds, hereafter obtained from the United States, on account of the claim of this Commonwealth, for disbursements made, and expenses incurred, for the defence of the State, during the late war with Great Britain, shall be received by this Commonwealth, and when received, shall be divided between the two States, in the proportion of two-thirds to this Commonwealth and one-third to the new State.

Fourth. All other property, of every description, belonging to the Commonwealth, shall be holden and receivable by the same, as a fund and security, for all debts, annuities, and Indian subsidies, or claims due by said Commonwealth; and within two years after the said District shall have become a separate State, the Commissioners to be appointed, as hereinafter provided, if the said States cannot otherwise agree, shall assign a just portion of the productive property so held by said Commonwealth, as an equivalent and indemnification to said Commonwealth, for all such debts and annuities, or Indian subsidies or claims, which may then remain due or unsatisfied; and all the surplus of the said property, so holden, as aforesaid, shall be divided between the said Commonwealth and the said District of Maine, in the proportion of two-thirds to the said Commonwealth, and one-third to the said District. And if, in the judgment of the said Commissioners, the whole of said property, so held, as a fund and security, shall not be sufficient indemnification, the said District shall be liable for, and shall pay to said Commonwealth, one-third of the deficiency.

Fifth. The new State shall, as soon as the necessary arrangements can be made for that purpose, assume and perform all the duties and obligations of this Commonwealth, towards the Indians within said District of Maine, whether the same arise from treaties, or otherwise; and for this purpose, shall obtain the assent of said Indians, and their release to this Commonwealth of claims and stipulations arising under the treaty at present existing between the said Commonwealth and said Indians; and as an indemnification to such new State, therefor, this Commonwealth, when such arrangements, shall be completed, and the said duties and obligations assumed, shall pay to said new State, the value of *thirty thousand dollars*, in manner following, viz: The said Commissioners shall set off by metes and bounds, so much of any part of the land, within the said District, falling to this Commonwealth, in the division of the public lands, hereinafter provided for, as in their estimation shall be of the value of thirty thousand dollars; and this

Commonwealth shall, thereupon, assign the same to the said new State; or in lieu thereof, may pay the sum of thirty thousand dollars, at its election; which election of the said Commonwealth, shall be made within one year from the time that notice of the doings of the Commissioners, on this subject, shall be made known to the Governor and Council; and if not made within that time, the election shall be with the new State.

Sixth. Commissioners, with the powers and for the purposes mentioned in this act, shall be appointed in manner following: The Executive authority of each State shall appoint two; and the four so appointed, or the major part of them, shall appoint two more; but if they cannot agree in the appointment, the Executive of each State shall appoint one in addition; not, however, in that case, to be a citizen of its own State. And any vacancy happening with respect to these two Commissioners, shall be supplied in the manner provided for their original appointment; and, in addition to the powers hereinbefore given to said Commissioners, they shall have full power and authority, and it shall be their duty, within ten years, next after the commissions shall be filled up, to divide all the public lands within the District, between the respective States, in equal shares, or moieties, in severalty, having regard to quantity, situation and quality; they shall determine what lands shall be surveyed and divided, from time to time; the expense of which surveys and of the commission, shall be borne equally by the two States. They shall keep fair records of their doings, and of the surveys made by their direction; copies of which records, authenticated by them, shall be deposited from time to time, in the archives of the respective States; transcripts of which, properly certified, may be admitted in evidence, in all questions touching the subject to which they relate. The Executive authority of each State may revoke the power of either or both its Commissioners; having, however, first appointed a substitute or substitutes, and may fill any vacancy happening with respect to its own Commissioners; four of said Commissioners shall constitute a quorum, for the transaction of business; their decision shall be final, upon all subjects within their cognizance. In case said commission shall expire, the division not having been completed, and either State shall request the renewal or filling up of the same, it shall be renewed, or filled up in the same manner as is herein provided for filling the same, in the first instance, and with the like powers; and if either state shall, after six months' notice, neglect or refuse to appoint its Commissioners, either for filling the commission in the first instance, or the renewal thereof, the other may fill up the whole commission.

Seventh. All grants of land, franchises, immunities, corporate or other rights, and all contracts for, or grants of land not yet located, which have been or may be made by the said Commonwealth, before the separation of said District shall take place, having or to have effect within the said District, shall continue in full force, after the said District shall become a separate State. But the grant which has been made to the President and Trustees of Bowdoin College, out of the tax laid upon the banks, within this Commonwealth, shall be charged upon the tax upon the banks within the said District of Maine, and paid according to the terms of said grant; and the President and Trustees, and the Overseers of said College, shall have, hold and enjoy their powers and privileges in all respects; so that the same shall not be subject to be altered, limited, annulled or restrained, except by judicial process, according to the principles of law; and in all grants hereafter to be made, by either State, of unlocated land within the said District, the same reservations shall be made for the benefit of schools and of the ministry, as have heretofore been usual, in grants made by this Commonwealth. And all lands heretofore granted by this Commonwealth, to any religious, literary, or eleemosynary corporation, or society, shall be free from taxation, while the same continues to be owned by such corporation, or society.

Eighth. No laws shall be passed in the proposed State, with regard to taxes, actions or remedies at law, or bars, or limitations thereof, or otherwise making any distinction between the lands and rights of property of proprietors, not residents in, or not citizens of said proposed State, and the lands and rights of property of the citizens of the proposed State, resident therein; and the rights and liabilities of all persons, shall, after the said separation, continue the same as if the said District was still a part of this Commonwealth, in all suits pending, or judgments remaining unsatisfied, on the fifteenth day of March next where the suits have been commenced in Massachusetts proper, and process has been served within the District of Maine; or commenced in the District of Maine, and process has been served in Massachusetts proper, either by taking bail, making attachments, arresting and detaining persons, or otherwise, where execution remains to be done; and in such suits, the courts within Massachusetts proper, and within the proposed State, shall continue to have the same jurisdiction as if the said District still remained a part of the Commonwealth. And this Commonwealth shall have the same remedies, within the proposed State, as it now has, for the collection of all taxes, bonds or debts, which may be assessed, due, made, or contracted, by, to, or with the Commonwealth, on or before the said fifteenth day of March within the said District of Maine; and all officers within Massachusetts proper and the District of Maine, shall conduct themselves accordingly.

Ninth. These terms and conditions, as here set forth, when the said District shall become a separate and independent State, shall, *ipso facto*, be incorporated into, and become, and be a part of any constitution, provisional, or other, under which the government of the said proposed State shall, at any time hereafter, be administered; subject, however, to be modified, or annulled, by the agreement of the Legislature of both the said States; but by no other power or body whatsoever.

SECT. 2. *Be it further enacted,* That the inhabitants of the several towns, districts, and plantations, in the District of Maine, qualified to vote for Governor or Senators, shall assemble in regular meeting, to be notified by warrants of the proper officers, on the fourth Monday of July next, and shall, in open meeting, give in their votes, on this question: "Is it expedient, that the District of Maine shall become a separate and independent State, upon the terms and conditions, provided in an act, entitled "An act relating to the separation of the District of Maine from Massachusetts proper, and forming the same into a separate and independent State?" And the selectmen of the towns and districts, and the assessors of the plantations, shall, in open meeting, receive, sort, count and declare, and the clerks thereof, respectively, shall record the votes given for and against the measure; and the said selectmen, assessors, and clerks, respectively, shall make out an exact return thereof, under their hands and shall seal up and transmit the same to the office of the Secretary of this Commonwealth, on or before the fourth Monday of August next. And all returns, not then made, shall be rejected in the counting; and the Governor and Council shall open and examine the said returns, made as aforesaid, and shall count the votes given on the said question; and the Governor shall, by public proclamation, to be made as soon as the state of the vote can be ascertained, after the said fourth Monday of August next, make known the result, by declaring the number of votes appearing in favor of the separation of said District, as aforesaid, and the number of votes appearing against it. And, if the number of votes for the measure shall exceed the number of votes against it, by fifteen hundred, then, and not otherwise, the people of said District shall be deemed to have expressed their consent and agreement, that the said District shall become a separate and independent State, upon the terms and conditions above stated; and in case of such majority, the Governor, in his said proclamation, shall call upon the people of said District to choose delegates to meet in convention for the purposes, and, in the manner hereinafter provided; and, in addition to publishing said proclamation, in one or more of the public newspapers printed in Boston, and in the District of Maine, copies of the same, duly authenticated, shall, as soon as can conveniently be done, after the making of the same, be transmitted to the office of the clerks of the courts of Common Pleas, in the several counties of the District of Maine, for public examination; and one such copy, at least, shall be transmitted to the convention of delegates, hereinafter mentioned, when said convention shall be formed.

SECT. 3. *Be it further enacted,* That if it shall be declared by said proclamation, that the said majority of fifteen hundred votes appeared by the said returns to be in favor of the separation of the said District as aforesaid; the inhabitants of the several towns and districts, now entitled to send one or more Representatives to the General Court, and all other incorporated towns, shall, on the third Monday of September next, assemble in town meeting, to be notified by warrant of the selectmen, and shall elect one or more delegates (not exceeding the number of representatives which such town is now entitled to; each town, however, to be at liberty to elect at least one,) to meet delegates from other towns within the said District, in convention, for the purpose of forming a constitution, or frame of government, for the said District. And at such meeting of the said inhabitants, every person qualified to vote for Senators, shall have a right to vote in the choice of delegates. And the selectmen shall preside, at such meeting, and shall in open meeting, receive, sort, count and declare the votes, and the clerk shall make a record thereof, in presence of the selectmen, and in open meeting. And fair copies of the said records shall be attested by the selectmen and town clerk, and one such copy shall be delivered by the selectmen to each of the persons duly elected a delegate.

SECT. 4. *Be it further enacted*, That the persons so elected delegates, shall meet in convention, at the Court House, in Portland, in the County of Cumberland, on the second Monday of October next, and they shall be the judges of the returns and election of their own members, and may adjourn from time to time, and sixty of the persons elected shall constitute a quorum for the transaction of business; and the said delegates shall, as soon as may be, proceed to organize themselves, in convention, by choosing a President, and such other officers as they may judge expedient, and establishing proper rules of proceedings; and it shall be the duty of the said convention, to apply to the Congress of the United States for its assent to be given, before the last day of January next, that the said District should be admitted into the Union, as a separate and independent State. And it shall also be the duty of the said convention, to form a constitution, or frame of government, for said new State, and to determine the style and title of the same; and such constitution, when adopted, and ratified by the people of said District, in the manner hereinafter mentioned, shall, from and after the fifteenth day of March, in the year of our Lord, one thousand eight hundred and twenty, (the consent of the Congress of the United States, then being first had, as aforesaid,) be the constitution of said new State. And the said convention shall, as soon as may be, after having formed such constitution, or frame of government, for such new State, cause the same to be published, and sent to the several towns, districts, and plantations, within the said District of Maine; and there shall be a meeting of the inhabitants, in each of said towns, districts, and plantations, to be called and warned by the selectmen, and assessors respectively, in due course of law; and on the day named by said convention, at which meeting, every male inhabitant, having the personal qualifications, herein declared requisite in the election of delegates to said convention, shall have a right to vote; and the people so assembled, shall give in their votes in writing, expressing their approbation or disapprobation of the constitution so prepared, and proposed by said convention. And the selectmen of the several towns, and the assessors of the several districts, and plantations respectively, shall preside at such meetings, and shall receive the votes of all the inhabitants, duly qualified as aforesaid, and shall sort and count them in open meeting of the town, district, or plantation; and the same shall be then and there recorded in the books of the town, district, or plantation; and a fair copy of such record shall be attested by the selectmon or assessors, and the clerk of the town, district, or plantation, respectively, and shall be, by the said selectmen or assessors, transmitted and delivered to the said convention, or to the President thereof, for the time being, or to any committee appointed to receive the same, on or before the first day of January next; on which day, or within ten days thereafter, the said convention shall be in session, and shall receive and count all the votes returned, and declare and publish the result; and if a majority of the votes so returned, shall be in favor of the constitution proposed, as aforesaid, the said constitution shall go into operation, according to its own provisions; otherwise the constitution of Massachusetts, with the addition of the terms and conditions herein provided, shall be, and be considered as the constitution of the said proposed State, in manner as hereafter provided. And to the end, that no period of anarchy may happen to the people of said proposed State, in case a new constitution shall not be so adopted and ratified by the people of said District of Maine, the present constitution of the Commonwealth of Massachusetts, shall, with the terms and conditions aforesaid, and with the exception hereinafter made, be provisionally, the constitution or frame of government, for said District; except only such parts of said constitution of Massachusetts, as relate to the style or title of said State, or may be otherwise inconsistent with, or repugnant to the situation and condition of said new State; and except, that the people of said District shall choose in their senatorial districts, as now established, three times the number of Senators now allowed them, and that the Legislature shall choose such a number of councilors, not exceeding nine, as they shall determine to be proper. And the said convention shall designate the place for the first meeting of the Legislature of said new State, and for the organization of its government, and shall appoint a Secretary, pro tempore, for said new State; and the said convention shall regulate the pay of its members; and the person, authorized by said convention, may draw upon the treasury of the Commonwealth for the amount of the money paid into the treasury by the several banks within said District, for the tax upon the same, due and payable on the first Monday of October next; and the sum or sums so drawn for, and paid out of the treasury, shall be a charge upon the new State in the division of the property, provided for in the fourth article of the terms and conditions stated in the first section of this act.

SECT. 5. *Be it further enacted,* That until a Governor of the proposed State shall be chosen and qualified according to the constitution which may be in operation in said State, the person last chosen President of the said convention, shall, from and after the fifteenth day of March next, have all the power of the Governor and Council under the constitution of Massachusetts, until a new Governor shall be chosen and qualified in the said proposed State; excepting only, that the said President shall not have the power to remove from office any officer who may be duly qualified, and executing the duties of his office according to the intent and meaning of this act. And in order that there may be no failure of justice, and that no danger may arise to the people of the said District of Maine, after the fifteenth day of March next, and before the government of the said State shall be fully organized; therefore,

SECT. 6. *Be it further enacted,* That all the laws which shall be in force within the said District of Maine, upon the said fifteenth day of March next, shall still remain, and be in force, within the said proposed State, until altered or repealed by the government thereof, such parts only excepted as may be inconsistent with the situation and condition of said new State, or repugnant to the constitution thereof. And all officers, who shall, on the said fifteenth day of March next, hold commissions, or exercise any authority within the said District of Maine, under the Commonwealth of Massachusetts, or by virtue of the laws thereof, excepting only, the Governor, Lieutenant Governor and Council, the members of the Legislature, and the Justices of the Supreme Judicial Court of the said Commonwealth of Massachusetts, shall continue to have, hold, use, exercise and enjoy, all the powers and authority to them respectively granted or committed, until other persons shall be appointed in their stead, or until their respective offices shall be annulled by the government of said proposed State. And all courts of law, whatsoever, within the said proposed State, excepting only the Supreme Judicial Court, shall proceed to hear and determine all causes, matters and things, which are or may be commenced or depending before them, respectively, upon the said fifteenth day of March next, or at any time afterwards, and before the government of the said proposed State shall establish new courts within the same; and shall continue from and after the said fifteenth day of March next, to exercise the like power and authority, and in like manner as they now by law may do, until such new courts shall be so established, in their stead.

SECT. 7. *Be it further enacted,* That all actions, suits, and causes, civil and criminal, and all matters and things whatsoever, that shall, on the said fifteenth day of March next, be in any manner depending in the Supreme Judicial Court of the said

Commonwealth of Massachusetts, then last holden within any county in the said District of Maine, and all writs, recognizances and other processes whatsoever, that may then be returnable to the said Supreme Judicial Court, shall be respectively transferred, and returned to, have day in, and be heard, tried, and determined in the highest court of law that shall be established in the said new State, by the government thereof; and at the first term of such court, that shall be held within the county in which such action, writ, process, or other matter or thing, may be so pending or returnable. And in all cases of appeals from any Circuit Court of Common Pleas, or Probate, or other court, which shall be made after the said fifteenth day of March next, in any action, cause, or suit whatsoever, and which would by law be made to the said Supreme Judicial [Court] thereof, it shall be sufficient for the appellant to claim an appeal, without naming or designating the court appealed to; and such appeal shall be entered at the Supreme or Superior Judicial Court, or highest court of law, to be established by the government of the said new State, which shall first thereafter be held within or for the county in which such action, cause, or suit, may be pending, and shall there be heard, tried, and determined, according to law. *Provided, however,* That nothing contained in this section shall be understood or construed to control, in any degree, the right of the people of the said new State, or the government thereof, to establish judicial courts, in such manner, and with such authority as they shall see fit; nor to prevent the said people or their government from making any other provisions, pursuant to their constitution, and not repugnant to the terms and conditions above set forth, respecting all the said actions, suits, processes, matters and things, herein above mentioned, as they shall think most proper, to prevent the discontinuance thereof, and to avoid any delay or failure of justice.

[Approved by the Governor, June 19th, 1819.]

COMMONWEALTH OF MASSACHUSETTS.

The Committee of Council appointed to examine the returns of the votes from the several towns and plantations in the District of Maine, relative to the separation of that District from Massachusetts proper, and to report thereon; respectfully state, that they have attended to that service, and find the following result, viz:

Counties.	Whole number.	For separation.	Against separation.
Cumberland,	4,709	3,315	1,394
Hancock,	1,581	820	761
Kennebec,	4,591	3,950	641
Lincoln,	4,057	2,523	1,534
York,	3,732	2,086	1,646
Oxford,	2,443	1,893	550
Penobscot,	815	584	231
Washington,	618	480	138
Somerset,	1,677	1,440	237
Total,	24,223	17,091	7,132

They therefore ask leave to report, that the whole number of votes, legally returned, are twenty-four thousand two hundred and twenty-three; of which seventeen thousand and ninety-one are in favor of separation; and seven thousand one hundred and thirty-two against it; making the majority in favor of separation nine thousand nine hundred and fifty-nine.

The committee further report, that they have rejected only one return, which stated that there were ninety-one votes in favor of separation and none against it; but neither the name of the town or county appeared on the face of the return, though by a writing on the outside, unsigned, it was stated to be from Newport, in the County of Penobscot; and there were no returns from the following towns and plantations: In Kennebec County, from Temple—in Cumberland, from Thompson pond plantation—in Hancock, from Sullivan, and from Mariaville plantation—in Somerset, from Moscow and from Sebasticook plantation—from Snake Root Hill plantation—from plantations No. 3, west of Kennebec River, and No. 3, east of said River—in Penobscot, from plantation No. 3, 6th Range, Williamsburgh plantation, and plantation No. 4, 2d Range—in York, from Arundel and Limerick—in Oxford, from plantation No. 4, from Brackley's grant, and Lunt's grant—in Washington, from Addison, Cobb's Cook or plantation No. 9, and Little Machias or plantation No. 11.

All which is respectfully submitted.

BENJA. PICKMAN, *Per Order*.

COUNCIL CHAMBER, August 24, 1819.

IN COUNCIL, August 24th, 1819.

This Report is accepted.

A. BRADFORD, *Sec'y of Commonwealth*.

Copy. Examined by

ALDEN BRADFORD, *Sec'y of Commonwealth*.

PROCLAMATION.

COMMONWEALTH OF MASSACHUSETTS.

By His Excellency John Brooks,
Governor of the Commonwealth of Massachusetts:

A PROCLAMATION.

Whereas by an act of the Legislature of this Commonwealth passed on the nineteenth day of June last, entitled "An act relating to the separation of the District of Maine from Massachusetts proper, and forming the same into a separate and independent State" it is among other things provided, that the inhabitants of the several towns, districts and plantations, in the District of Maine, qualified to vote for Governor or Senators, should assemble in regular meeting to be notified by warrants of the proper officers, on the fourth Monday of July then next, and in open meeting give in their votes on this question,

"Is it expedient that the District of Maine shall become a separate and independent State upon the terms and conditions provided in the act aforesaid?"

And whereas provision is made by said act for the return of the votes so given, both for and against the measure, into the office of the Secretary of this Commonwealth, on or before the fourth Monday of August then next and for the opening, examining and counting of said votes by the Governor and Council;

And whereas it is further provided in said act, that as soon after the said fourth Monday of August as the state of said votes could be ascertained, the Governor should, by public proclamation, make known the result by declaring the number of votes appearing in favor of the separation of said District as aforesaid, and the number of votes appearing against it; and in case the number of votes for the measure should exceed the number of votes against it by fifteen hundred, that the Governor should in his said proclamation, call upon the people of said

District to choose delegates to meet in convention for the purposes expressed and in the manner prescribed in said Act;

Now therefore I, JOHN BROOKS, Governor of the Commonwealth of Massachusetts, do hereby declare and make known, to all whom it may concern, that upon a careful examination in manner aforesaid, of all the votes for and against said measure, duly and legally returned into the Secretary's [Office] conformably to said Act, it appears, that the whole number of votes given in favor of the separation of said District as aforesaid was seventeen thousand and ninety-one, and that the whole number of votes against it was seven thousand one hundred and thirty-two.

And inasmuch as the number of votes for said measure exceeds the number of votes against it by fifteen hundred and upwards, I do hereby, by virtue of the authority given and pursuant to the requisitions contained in said Act, call upon the inhabitants of the several towns and districts now entitled to send one or more representatives to the General Court, and all other incorporated towns in said District of Maine, to assemble in town meeting in their respective towns on the third Monday of September next, to be notified by warrant of the selectmen and elect one or more delegates not exceeding the number of representatives which such town is now entitled to, (each town, however, to be at liberty to elect one,) to meet delegates from other towns within the said District, in convention, at the Court House in Portland, in the County of Cumberland, on the second Monday of October next, for the purpose of forming a constitution or frame of government for the said District, and for other purposes expressed in said Act.

Given under my hand and the seal of the Commonwealth at Boston, this twenty-fourth day of August A. D. eighteen hundred and nineteen; and in the forty-fourth year of the independence of the United States of America.

[L. S.]

JOHN BROOKS.

By His Excellency the Governor:

ALDEN BRADFORD, *Sec'y of the Commonwealth.*

Copy. Examined by

ALDEN BRADFORD, *Sec'y of the Commonwealth.*

CONSTITUTIONAL CONVENTION.

DISTRICT OF MAINE.

PORTLAND,
MONDAY, October 11, 1819.

Agreeably to the provisions of the act of the Legislature of the Commonwealth of Massachusetts passed June 19, 1819, entitled "An act relating to the separation of the District of Maine from Massachusetts proper, and forming the same into a separate and independent State," the delegates therein mentioned assembled at the Court House in Portland, when the Honorable Daniel Cony was by vote unanimously requested to act as Chairman, who after addressing the delegates took the Chair.

On motion, *Voted*, That a committee of five be appointed to examine the credentials of members, when the Hon. John Holmes, Hon Albion K. Parris, Hon. Joshua Gage, Hon. Judah Dana, and William Abbott, Esquire, were appointed said committee.

On motion, *Voted unanimously*, That a Reverend member present be requested to offer prayers previous to proceeding to organize the convention, whereupon the Rev. Mr. Titcomb, of Brunswick, at the request of the Chairman, performed that duty.

The committee appointed to examine the credentials of the several members returned to this convention, made a report, by which it appeared, that there were two hundred and seventy-four members then present, which were legally returned, which report being read with the names of the members so returned, was accepted.

Voted, That a committee be appointed to collect, sort, and count, the votes for President—whereupon the Hon. Benjamin Greene, Hon. Ezekiel Whitman, Hon. James Bridge, Hon. Benjamin Ames and the Hon. James Campbell, were appointed,—the same committee, proceeded and made report, that they had performed the duties assigned, and find the whole number of votes to be two hundred and forty-one, of which, the Hon. WILLIAM KING has two hundred and thirty votes—which report was received and read from the chair, and the Hon. gentleman was declared to be duly elected; whereupon he was conducted to the Chair, and made his acknowledgments to the convention. The convention then proceeded to the choice of a Secretary, by ballot; and the votes being taken, it appeared that the whole number of votes given were two hundred and forty-three—necessary to a choice, one hundred and twenty-two; and no person appearing to have that number, the convention proceeded to a second ballot, when it appeared that the whole number of votes given in were two hundred and fifty-seven—necessary to make a choice, one hundred and twenty-nine; Robert C. Vose, Esq., had one hundred and sixty-six votes, and was chosen—who accepted of the choice.

DANIEL CONY, *Chairman.*

Resolved, That a Sergeant-at-Arms be appointed by the President, whose duty it shall be to execute the orders of the convention and to assist the President in the preservation of order, and he shall employ a doorkeeper, and such assistance as may be necessary; in pursuance of the above resolution, the President appointed Mr. William B. Peters, of Portland, to be Sergeant-at-Arms.

Resolved, That a committee consisting of three members be appointed to prepare and report proper rules of proceeding for this convention. The Hon. George Thatcher, Hon. Benjamin Greene and the Hon. James Campbell, were appointed on the said committee.

Resolved, That the several ordained and settled clergymen of the town of Portland be requested by the Sergeant-at-Arms, in behalf of this convention, from day to day in succession, according to seniority, to attend and perform the duties of chaplain to this convention.

Resolved, That the President assign to any editor of any public newspaper, or the agent of any such editor, who may apply for it, a convenient situation for the purpose of taking notes of the proceedings of the convention.

Resolved, That a Committee of Election be appointed, consisting of five members.

Voted, That when the convention do adjourn, that it adjourn to meet in the meeting-house of the First Parish in Portland which had been previously prepared for the use of the convention.

Adjourned to 9 o'clock to-morrow morning.

TUESDAY, OCTOBER 12, 1819.

Met according to adjournment.

The committee appointed to prepare rules and orders having attended to the duty assigned them, made a report which was read and accepted as amended, and ordered to be printed with a list of the members and the general committees which have been appointed.

Ordered, That the wall pews on the southeast side of the meetinghouse be appropriated for the use of such spectators as may be invited to a seat by any of the members of this convention.

The following resolutions submitted by the Hon. Mr. Parris, were taken up and accepted as amended:

Resolved, That a committee consisting of thirty-three members, be appointed to prepare and report to this convention, a constitution or frame of government for the new State, agreeably to the fourth section of the act of the Legislature of the Commonwealth of Massachusetts, passed June 19th, 1819, entitled "An act relating to the separation of the District of Maine from Massachusetts proper, and forming the same into a separate and independent State."

Ordered, That said committee be selected in manner following, viz: From the counties of York, Cumberland, Lincoln and Kennebec, five each; from the counties of Oxford, Somerset and Hancock, three each; and from the counties of Penobscot and Washington, two each.

Resolved, That a committee consisting of five members, be appointed to prepare and report to this convention an application to the Congress of the United States, for its assent to be given before the last day of January next, that the District of Maine be admitted into the Union as a separate and independent State.

Resolved, That the foregoing committees be nominated by the President and appointed by the convention.

Resolved, That a committee of nine members be appointed to consider and report to this convention a proper style and title for the new State.

Resolved, That the Secretary be authorized to appoint Assistants or Clerks to assist him in the duties of his office.

Voted, That when the convention do adjourn, it be until 4 o'clock this afternoon. Adjourned.

AFTERNOON.

Met. Several packages, addressed to the convention, purporting to be from the Secretary's Office of the Commonwealth of Massachusetts, were received and ordered to lie upon the table.

Ordered, That the returns of the several members to this convention, be committed to the Committee on Elections, and the remonstrance of Nathan Shaw and others, against the election of Samuel Davis, to the same committee.

Ordered, That the Sergeant-at-Arms be directed to provide a suitable room for the accommodation of the committee on the subject of framing the constitution.

The President appointed the following committee on the constitution of the new State:

YORK.

Hon. Mr. Holmes of Alfred; Mr. Dane of Wells; Hon. Mr. Moody of Saco; Hon. Mr. Rice of Kittery; Mr. Marston of Parsonsfield.

CUMBERLAND.

Hon. Judge Parris, Hon. Mr. Whitman of Portland; Hon. Mr. Lewis of Gorham; Mr. Foxcroft of New Gloucester; Hon. Mr. Page of Brunswick.

LINCOLN.

Gen. Wingate of Bath; Mr. Dole of Alna; Mr. Head of Waldoboro'; Mr. Rose of Boothbay; Mr. Neal of Litchfield.

KENNEBEC.

Hon. Mr. Chandler of Monmouth; Judge Bridge of Augusta;

Rev. Mr. Francis of Leeds; Mr. Redington of Vassalboro'; Gen. Wellington of Fairfax.

HANCOCK.

Mr. Johnson of Belfast; Rev. Mr. Hall of Frankfort; Mr. Johnson of Jackson.

OXFORD.

Hon. Judge Dana of Fryeburg; Rev. Mr. Hooper of Paris; Gen. Turner of Turner.

SOMERSET.

Gen. Kendall of Fairfield; Mr. Allen of Norridgewock; Mr. Baldwin of Mercer.

PENOBSCOT.

Major Treat of Bangor; Mr. Wilkins of Orrington.

WASHINGTON.

Hon. Mr. Campbell of Harrington; Mr. Dickinson of Machias.

COMMITTEE ON THE STYLE AND TITLE OF THE NEW STATE.

Mr. Preble of Portland; Mr. Allen of Sanford; Mr. Wood of Wiscasset; Mr. Cutler of Farmington; Mr. Stetson of Hampden; Mr. Abbot of Castine; Mr. Chandler of Parris; Mr. French of St. Albans; and Mr. Vance of Calais.

COMMITTEE ON ELECTIONS.

Hon. Judge Thatcher of Biddeford; Mr. Emery of Portland; Mr. Burnham of Unity; Mr. Vergin of Rumford; Mr. Dearborn of Hallowell.

COMMITTEE TO MAKE APPLICATION TO CONGRESS.

Hon. Judge Greene of South Berwick; Hon. Judge Cony of Augusta; Hon. Judge Ames of Bath; Mr. Jarvis of Surry; Hon. Mr. Clapp of Portland.

Resolved, That a committee of three members be appointed on leave of absence of members. Mr. Moody of Hallowell, Mr. Herrick of Bowdoinham, and Mr. Wood of Lebanon, were appointed said committee.

Resolved, That a committee of three members be appointed on the pay roll. Gen. Irish of Gorham, Mr. Thatcher of Saco, and Col. Reed of Waldoboro', were appointed said committee.

Voted, That when the convention adjourn, it be until 10 o'clock to-morrow morning. Adjourned accordingly.

WEDNESDAY, OCTOBER 13, 1819.

Met according to adjournment.

The remonstrance of David Curtis and others, against the election of Joseph Neally, read and committed to the Committee on Elections.

Ordered, That the Committee on Elections have leave to set in committee, during the time the convention may be in session; and that the member from the town of Dearborn, have leave to attest as Town Clerk of said Dearborn, the certificate of his election, now in the hands of the Committee on Elections; and that the same indulgence be given to other members of this convention who may have been returned under similar circumstances.

Resolved, That a committee of three members be appointed to take into consideration and report upon the necessary expenditures of this convention exclusive of the pay roll. The Hon. Mr. Gage of Augusta, Mr. Shepley of Saco, and Mr. Ilsley of Portland, were appointed on the said committee.

Leave of absence, (reported by the committee,) was given to Mr. Burr of Litchfield, Mr. McCobb of Phipsburg, and Mr. McLellan of Gray, until Monday next.

Resolved, That Col. Trescott of Lubec, Mr. Wallingford of Saco, and Commodore Tucker of Bristol, be a committee to consider and report what further acts, resolves and other documents it may be proper to obtain from the office of the Secretary of the Commonwealth of Massachusetts.

Adjourned to 4 o'clock this afternoon.

AFTERNOON.

Met. The petition of Samuel Haywood and others, inhabitants of Sidney—read and committed to the committee who have under consideration the subject of preparing a constitution or frame of government for the new State.

Resolved, That a committee consisting of nine members be appointed to take into consideration, what compensation shall be allowed the members of this convention for their travel and attendance. Mr. Low of Lyman, Mr. Adams of Gorham, Mr. Spear of Thomaston, Mr. Lock of Chesterville, Col. Steele of Brownfield, Mr. Tuttle of Canaan, Col. Atherton of Prospect, Mr. Leonard of Brewer, and Mr. Burgin of Eastport, were appointed on the said committee.

Resolved, That Henry Smith, Esq., of Portland, be appointed and authorized to draw upon the Treasurer of the Commonwealth of Massachusetts, for the amount of the pay roll for the travel and attendance of the members of the convention; *provided* the same does not exceed the amount of the money paid into the treasury by the several banks, within this District, for the tax upon the same due and payable the first Monday of October instant.

Ordered, That the motion made by Mr. Herrick of Bowdoinham, on the subject of arranging the seats of the members, be committed to the committee on the rules and proceedings of this convention.

Mr. Preble of Portland, chairman of the committee appointed on the subject of the style and title for the new State, made a report, which was read; and on motion of Mr. Dearborn of Hallowell, was assigned for consideration, to-morrow, at 10 o'clock.

Voted, That when the convention adjourn it be until 10 o'clock to-morrow morning.

Adjourned accordingly.

THURSDAY, OCTOBER 14, 1819.

Met according to adjournment.

Agreeably to assignment, the report of the committee made yesterday upon the subject of the style and title of the new State, was taken up, and a motion made by Mr. Parsons of Edgecomb, that the word "Commonwealth" be stricken out; and, after much debate, the motion was carried, 119 members voting in the affirmative, and 113 in the negative. A motion was then made that the word "State" be inserted in place of the word "Commonwealth," which had been stricken out, which motion passed in the affirmative without division. On motion of Judge Ames, the report was further postponed, and the convention adjourned to 3 o'clock this afternoon.

AFTERNOON.

Met. Mr. Milliken of Frankfort, presented the remonstrance of John Hull the 2d, and others, against the election of Samuel A. Whitney, Esq., of Lincolnville; Judge Thatcher presented the remonstrance of Nathan Hanson and others, against the election of Henry Norton, Esq., of New Portland; and Mr. Dickinson of Machias, presented the remonstrance of Isaac Keen and others, against the election of William Vance, Esq., of Calais—which were severally read and committed to the Committee on Elections.

The Committee on Elections, made a report, which was read and recommitted to the same committee who reported it; and ordered that said committee be instructed to examine all the returns of members of this convention, and report who and what members of the convention are duly elected, and who are not duly elected, and the reasons thereof.

The Hon. Mr. Holmes, Chairman of the Committee appointed to prepare and report to this convention a constitution or frame of government for the new State, made a report in part, which was read, and Monday next, at 12 o'clock, was assigned for taking the same into consideration—and ordered that 500 copies of this report be printed for the use of the members.

The resolution submitted yesterday, by Mr. Kingsbery of Gardiner, was taken up and passed, as follows:

Resolved, That the Hon. Mr. Clapp and Mr. Ilsley of Portland, and Mr. Dearborn of Hallowell, be a Committee of Finance to devise ways and means to defray the expenses of this convention, should the amount exceed the sum to be received from the Treasurer of the Commonwealth of Massachusetts.

On motion of Mr. Wallingford of Wells, the committee appointed yesterday to consider and report what further acts, resolves, and other documents, it may be necessary to obtain from the Secretary's Office of the Commonwealth of Massachusetts, were authorized to inquire into the expediency of applying to the office of the Secretary of the United States, for any documents in his department, which may be required for the new State.

Adjourned to 10 o'clock to-morrow morning.

FRIDAY, October 15, 1819.

Met according to adjournment.

Ordered, That so much of the report of the committee appointed to prepare and report a constitution or frame of government for the new State, as relates to the style and title, be stricken out whenever it occurs, and that the secretary be directed so to amend said report.

Col. Atherton of Prospect, presented the petition of Phinehas Varnum and others, officers of the second brigade and twelfth division of the Militia, which was read and committed to the committee appointed to prepare and report a constitution.

Mr. Bradbury of York, was appointed on the committee upon the subject of the pay of members, in place of Mr. Low of Lyman, who is absent.

The convention resumed the consideration of the report of the committee upon the subject of the style and title of the new state. A motion was made by Judge Cony, further to amend the same by striking out the word "Maine," and to insert, in lieu thereof, "Columbus"; after much debate, the question was put and decided in the negative; the ordinance determining the style and title of the new State, was then read and passed, as follows:

"An ordinance determining the style and title of the State."

"Be it ordained and determined by the delegates of the people, inhabiting the territory now called and known by the name of the District of Maine, in convention assembled,

That provided the District of Maine aforesaid, shall, before the fourth day of March next, be admitted into the Union as a separate and independent State on an equal footing with the original States, the said State shall be known and called by the style and title of the *State of Maine.* Done in convention this fifteenth day of October, in the year of our Lord one thousand eight hundred and nineteen."

Adjourned to 3 o'clock this afternoon.

AFTERNOON.

Met. On motion of Judge Greene of South Berwick,

Ordered, That all ordinances and resolves in the nature of ordinances, passed by this convention, be signed by the President of the convention, and attested by the Secretary.

The committee on the subject of the pay of the members for their travel and attendance, reported the following resolution, which was read and accepted:

Resolved, That there be allowed and paid to the members of this convention, as compensation for their travel and attendance, as follows, to wit: To each of said members two dollars for each twenty miles travel in going to, and returning from said convention, and to each of said members, two dollars for each day's attendance thereat.

Resolved, That Mr. Lock of Chesterville, Mr. Shepley of Saco, and Mr. Herrick of Bowdoinham, be a committee to consider and report upon the manner of receiving the returns from the selectmen of the several towns, and assessors of the several districts and plantations, of the votes which may be given in for or against the constitution which may be submitted to the people for their consideration and adoption.

Mr. Lamson of Wayne, presented the petition of James Wing and others, upon the subject of the Militia, which was read and committed to the committee who have under consideration the subject of the constitution.

Voted, That when the convention adjourn, it be till to-morrow morning at 10 o'clock. Adjourned accordingly.

SATURDAY, October 16, 1819.

Met according to adjournment.

Judge Thatcher, chairman of the Committee of Elections, made a report, that the committee have carefully examined the returns and certificates of the delegates returned from the several towns in the District of Maine, to this convention, and that said committee are of the opinion that the delegates from the following towns are severally entitled to their seats, viz: The delegates from all the towns in the county of York; also, from all the towns in the county of Cumberland, except the town of Standish; also, from all the towns in the county of Lincoln, except the town of Hope; also, from all the towns in the county of Hancock, except the towns of Ellsworth, Knox, Orland, Gouldsborough, Monroe and Lincolnville; also from all the towns in the county of Washington, except the town of Calais; also, from all the towns in the county of Kennebec, except the town of Rome; also, from all the towns in the county of Somerset, except the towns of New Portland, Anson, and Mercer; and from all the towns in the county of Penobscot—which report being read, was accepted.

The same committee further report, that as to the elections in the towns above excepted to, on account of defects in the certificates of returns delivered to the delegates and here produced to the convention, they find that the returns produced by the delegate from the town of Standish, in the County of Cumberland, is defective in this, that it is not attested by either or any of the selectmen of said town; and as to the returns from the towns of Bethel and Buckfield, in the County of Oxford, in addition to many of the smaller defects before mentioned, they are defective, in that they are not attested by the town clerks of their respective towns, nor is there any other date to the return from the town of Bethel, than the year of Independence of the United States, which is stated to be the forty-third; the return from the town of Hope, in the County of Lincoln, is defective in this, it is not attested by the town clerk; the return from the town of Rome, County of Kennebec, appears to be defective in most of the particular requisites of the law, though it is attested by the selectmen and town clerk; it does not appear by any express words or facts stated from which an implication can be made *what* county the town is in; it does not appear by any express words or facts stated from which an implication can be made on what occasion the meeting was called. It states simply "that agreeably to a warrant notified according to law by the subscribers, the inhabitants of Rome met and brought in their votes as follows, viz:

For James Philbrick, Esq., six votes.
For Capt. J. S. Colbath, twenty-three votes.
For Christopher Knight, one vote."

Then follow the signatures of the selectmen and the town clerk. The returns from the towns of Knox and Orland, in the County of Hancock, are not attested by the selectmen of their respective towns, and the return from the town of Ellsworth is not signed by the town clerk of said town.

The returns from the towns of Anson and Mercer, in the county of Somerset, are defective in that they are not signed or attested by their respective Town Clerks. Which report being read, it was thereupon

Resolved, That the several members returned from the several towns of Standish, Bethel, Buckfield, Hope, Rome, Knox, Ellsworth, Orland, Anson and Mercer, are severally entitled to their seats in this convention, notwithstanding the defect or defects which may have appeared in their several returns.

The same committee reported that they had considered the remonstrance of Samuel Durgen and others, inhabitants of the town of Monroe, in the county of Hancock, against the election of Joseph Neally returned a delegate from said town to the convention, and submitted a statement of facts which was read, and the committee further submitted the following resolution:

Resolved, That the said Joseph Neally is entitled to his seat in this convention—which resolve was read and accepted.

The same committee further reported that they had considered the remonstrance of Jonathan Fernald and others, inhabitants of the town of Gouldsborough, against the election of Samuel Davis who is returned a delegate by said town; the committee submitted a statement of facts, and the following resolution:

Resolved, That the said Samuel Davis is entitled to a seat in this convention, which resolve was read and accepted.

The same committee further reported that they had had under consideration, the remonstrance of Nathan Hanson and others, against the election of Henry Norton, Esq., a delegate from New Portland, in the county of Somerset; the committee submitted a statement of facts, and the following resolve:

Resolved, That the said Henry Norton, Esq., is entitled to his seat as a delegate from the town of New Portland, which report and resolve was read and accepted.

And the same committee further reported that they had considered the remonstrance of Daniel Lane and others against the election of William Vance, Esq., returned as a delegate from the town of Calais, in the county of Washington, and submit the following statement of facts: That the said William Vance, at the time of his election and ever since lived in plantation number six, and that on the day of said election and before, he did state to the inhabitants and voters of said Calais, that they might legally vote for a person not an inhabitant of said town, and that the said remonstrants believed the said statement made as aforesaid had a powerful effect on the voters; and they further state that said plantation number six, has never been organized, neither have the inhabitants been assessed by the assessors of Calais, which is the next adjacent town, nor in any manner borne their share of the public burthens; and they state that they consider that the qualifications of voters and those to be elected are the same, and that they deemed the admitting the said William Vance, Esq., to hold a seat in this convention as much an encroachment upon their rights, as if the inhabitants of plantation number six had attended said election and overpowered the inhabitants of Calais by their votes; these allegations were admitted by the said William Vance; there was no evidence before the committee, of any improper means made use of to obtain his election other than what are stated as aforesaid, or that there was any improper conduct on the part of said delegate. Judge Thatcher, then submitted the following resolution:

Resolved, That the said William Vance, Esq., is entitled to his seat in this convention, which statement and resolution were severally read and accepted.

Judge Parris, from the committee appointed to prepare and report a constitution for the new State, made a communication to the convention, that said committee would make a further report this afternoon at 5 o'clock.

Adjourned to 3 o'clock this afternoon.

AFTERNOON.

Met. Mr. Virgin of Rumford, moved a reconsideration of the vote taken in the morning relative to the seat of William Vance, Esq. After much debate, the question was put and decided in the negative—forty-five members voting for the reconsideration and one hundred and five against, so the motion was lost.

A further communication was received by Mr. Johnson of Belfast, from the Committee on the Constitution, informing the convention that said committee would not have it in their power to make the report this afternoon, and that the committee requested leave to have their report printed, previous to its being submitted to the convention. *Thereupon Resolved*, That said committee be authorized to cause five hundred copies of their report to be printed, and that Mr. Wood of Wiscasset, be appointed to make this resolution known to the committee.

Voted, That when the convention adjourn, it be until 10 o'clock on Monday next.

Adjourned accordingly.

MONDAY, October 18, 1819.

Met according to adjournment.

The Committee on Elections reported that they had examined the returns made of the delegate from the town of Dresden, in the County of Lincoln, and that in their opinion Isaac Lilley, Esq., is duly elected a delegate from said town, and it was thereupon

Resolved, That the said Isaac Lilley is entitled to a seat in this convention.

Agreeably to assignment, the report of the Committee on the Constitution, made on Thursday last, was taken up, but it appearing that the chairman and many of the members of the committee who made the report, were absent, the consideration of the subject was postponed, and the convention

Adjourned to 3 o'clock this afternoon.

AFTERNOON.

Met. *Resolved,* That Henry Smith, Esq., of Portland, be appointed, and he is hereby authorized to draw on the Treasurer of the Commonwealth of Massachusetts, to the full amount of the money paid in the treasury by the several banks within the District, for the tax upon the same, due and payable on the first Monday of the present month, agreeably to the authority vested in this convention by an act of the Legislature of said Commonwealth, passed June 19, 1819, entitled "An act relating to the separation of the District of Maine from Massachusetts proper, and forming the same into a separate and independent State," as the amount of the pay roll of this convention will exceed the amount of the tax on the banks, due and payable as aforesaid, which resolve was read and accepted.

The Hon. Mr. Holmes, Chairman of the Committee appointed to prepare and report a constitution or frame of government for the new State, made a further report accompanied by a bill, which was read, and ordered that to-morrow morning, at 10 o'clock, be assigned for further consideration of the same, and that so much of the said report as has not been printed, be printed for the use of the members.

The convention resumed the consideration of the subject of the preamble and Bill of Rights. The preamble was first taken up and passed with sundry amendments. The first and second sections of the first article of the Bill of Rights were severally read and passed; the third section was also taken up and read.

Voted, That when the convention adjourn, it be until 9 o'clock to-morrow morning.

Adjourned accordingly.

TUESDAY, October 19, 1819.

Met according to adjournment.

Judge Dana of Fryeburg, had leave of absence by reason of sickness in his family.

Mr. Dole of Alna, presented the memorial of the Catholic Church of Maine, which was read and ordered to lie upon the table.

The convention resumed the subject of the Bill of Rights, or first article of the constitution, the third section being under consideration, was accepted with amendments.

Voted, (Two-thirds of the members present in the affirmative) that the fifth article, second chapter, of the rules and proceedings, be so far altered and amended, as that a motion for reconsideration of any vote may be made immediately after such vote may have been declared by the President.

Voted, That when the convention adjourn, it be until half-past 2 o'clock this afternoon, and that half-past 2 o'clock be the time to meet in the afternoon of each day, until the further order of the convention.

Adjourned accordingly.

AFTERNOON.

Met. On motion of Gen. Chandler, the convention reconsidered their former vote, fixing the time of adjournment.

Voted, That the convention will continue in session until half-past 1, and then adjourn to meet at 3 o'clock in the afternoon, until the further order of the convention.

The Bill of Rights or first article of the constitution, being under consideration, and the same having been read by sections and passed upon with sundry amendments, the question was put: Will the convention accept the first part of the report of the committee, so far as relates to the adoption of the Preamble and Bill of Rights, or first article of the constitution, as amended?—which report was unanimously accepted.

Ordered, That the Hon. Mr. Holmes, Hon. Mr. Whitman, and Mr. Johnson of Belfast, be a revising committee, and that the Preamble or Bill of Rights, be committed to said committee, for their examination.

The amendments to the Preamble and Bill of Rights were taken up and passed upon as follows:

Hon. Mr. Holmes moved to amend by striking out in the first and second line, these words, "that part of Massachusetts denominated the District of"—which motion passed in the affirmative.

In the seventh line, on motion of the Hon. Mr. Holmes, the words, "Great Legislator," were stricken out, and the words, "Sovereign Ruler," substituted instead.

Mr. Stevens of China, moved to amend article one, section third, in the eighth line, by inserting after the word sentiments, "Nevertheless, every sect or denomination of christians ought to observe the Sabbath or Lord's day and keep up some sort of religious worship which to them shall seem most agreeable to the revealed will of God"—which motion was negatived.

Mr. Emery of Portland, moved to amend in the second line by inserting after the word right, "to exercise the duty," —which motion was negatived.

Hon. Mr. Whitman, then moved further to amend said section in the sixteenth line after the word trust, by inserting, "as the happiness of a people and the good order and preservation of civil government essentially depend upon piety, religion and morality; and as these cannot generally be diffused, but by the institution of the public worship of Almighty God and of public instruction in piety, religion and morality—therefore, to promote their happiness, and to secure good order and the preservation of their government, the Legislature shall have power, and are hereby authorized, by all suitable means to encourage and uphold the institutions of public worship, and of public instruction in the principles of piety, religion and morality"—which motion being put, was negatived.

Mr. Hobbs of Waterborough, moved further to amend said section in the seventeenth line, by inserting, after the word State, these words, "nor shall any one ever be obliged to pay any tax or rate for the building or repairing any meeting-house or place of worship"—which motion was negatived.

Col. Reed of Waldoborough, moved to amend section four, in the seventh and eighth lines, by inserting after the word capacity, these words, "or the qualifications of those who are candidates for the suffrages of the people"—which motion passed in the affirmative.

Hon. Mr. Holmes moved further to amend the fourth section, by striking out after the word fact, in the eleventh line to the end of the section, these words, "under the direction of the court"—which motion passed in the affirmative.

The Hon. Mr. Holmes then moved further to amend, by inserting after the word jury, in the tenth line, these words, "after having received the direction of the court," and insert after shall, "at their discretion"—which amendment passed in the affirmative.

Section fifth passed without amendment.

Section sixth, in the third line: Mr. Neal of Elliot, moved to amend after the word counsel, to insert "or either"—which motion passed in the affirmative.

The sixth section then passed.

Section seventh: Mr. Wallingford moved to strike out in the first and second lines these words, "in all cases of a criminal nature the rights of trial by jury shall be preserved and,"—which motion passed in the affirmative.

The Hon. Mr. Holmes then moved further to amend said section, by inserting after the word impeachment, in the fifth line, "or in such cases of offenses as are usually cognizable by justices of the peace,"—which motion also passed in the affirmative, and the section ordered to be so amended.

Judge Cony moved further to amend, by inserting after the word "provide" "by law"—which motion passed, and the seventh section passed as amended.

Sections eighth, ninth and tenth, passed without amendment, and section eleven was taken into consideration.

Mr. Baldwin moved to amend in the second line, by striking out these words, "ex post facto," and to insert in lieu thereof, the following: "Laws punishing acts committed before the existence of such laws, and by them only declared criminal, are oppressive, unjust, and incompatible with liberty; whereupon no such law shall ever be made or exist in this State"—which motion was negatived; and Mr. Wallingford moved further to amend in the third line, by striking out after the word contracts, to the end of the section—which motion was also negatived.

Section eleventh passed without amendment.

Sections twelfth, thirteenth, fourteenth, fifteenth, sixteenth, seventeenth, eighteenth and nineteenth, were then severally read and passed.

Section twentieth was then taken up, and Mr. Neal of Elliot, moved to amend in the fourth line, by inserting these words, "and the party claiming the right may be heard by himself and his counsel, or either"—which motion passed in the affirmative.

Section twenty-first was then considered; and Mr. Milliken of Frankfort, moved to amend the same in the first line after the word taken, by adding these words, "or shall individual services be required"—which motion was negatived, and the section passed without amendment.

Sections twenty-second, twenty-third and twenty-fourth, were severally read and passed; and the report as amended, was unanimously accepted.

The Committee on Elections reported that in their opinion Samuel A. Whitney, Esq., the sitting member from the town of

Lincolnville, in the county of Hancock, is entitled to his seat in this convention—which report was accepted.

Voted, That when the convention adjourn, it be until half past 8 o'clock to-morrow morning.

Adjourned accordingly.

WEDNESDAY, OCTOBER 20, 1819.

Met according to adjournment.

Col. Atherton of Prospect, submitted the following motion and resolution, which were severally read and ordered to lie upon the table: "No law shall be made by which any individual may be subjected to the performance of any militia duties, from which or a direct equivalent, any white male inhabitant of reputable character, and of the same age, is by a law of the State, exempted."

Resolved, That a committee of nine, one from each County, be appointed to take into consideration the expediency of locating the seat of government for ——— years, and to designate the place most suitable for this purpose, and also for the first meeting of the Legislature of the new State, and for the organization of its government; and that the said committee be instructed to report previous to the final question being taken on the acceptance of the whole constitution.

The constitution, reported by the committee on that subject, was taken into consideration.

The first section of the second article, being under consideration, the Hon. Mr. Holmes moved to amend the same, by inserting after the word "State," in the fourth line, the following: "for the term of three months next preceding any election"—which passed in the affirmative.

Mr. Shepley of Saco, then moved to insert in the third line, after guardianship, "those who have been convicted of any infamous crime and not pardoned"—which motion being put was decided in the negative.

Mr. Vance moved further to amend in the third line, after the word Indians, by inserting, "and Negroes"—which motion was negatived.

Gen. Chandler moved to amend in the fifth line by inserting after the word where, "he has," and to strike out in the sixth line, "is established"—which motion was withdrawn by the mover.

Mr. Thomas of Wells, moved to insert in the second line, after the word "paupers," "supported by any town"—which motion was negatived.

Hon. Mr. Whitman moved further to amend in the second line, after the word paupers, and insert "during the time they be supported, in whole or in part, at the public expense" —which motion was decided in the negative.

Mr. Herrick of Bowdoinham, moved further to amend the first section, by inserting at the end of the section the following: "Neither shall the residence of a student at any seminary of learning, entitle him to the right of suffrage in the town or plantation where such seminary is established"—which motion passed in the affirmative.

The first section was then passed as amended.

Second section was then taken into consideration.

Hon. Mr. Moody moved to strike out after the word "election" in the third line, to the end of the section—which motion was negatived, and the second section was then passed without amendment.

Section third. Mr. Dickinson of Machias, moved to insert at the end of the section the following: "and except when called into actual service"—which motion was negatived, and the third section afterwards passed as reported by the committee.

Fourth section. Mr. Cutler of Farmington, moved to amend by striking out "September," and in lieu thereof, to insert "October"—which was negatived.

Dr. Perkins of Weld, moved further to amend this section by striking out "second," and inserting in lieu thereof, "third" —which motion was negatived, and the section passed without amendment.

The first and second sections of the third article, were then taken up, and passed without division.

Article four, section one, was passed without amendment.

Section second was then taken into consideration.

Judge Thatcher moved to amend the same, by striking out in the second line, these words, "one hundred, nor more than two hundred members"—which motion, after much debate, was decided in the negative, ninety-nine members voting in favor, and one hundred and forty-nine against the motion.

Mr. Kingsbury then moved to strike out the following words in the second, third and fourth lines: "to be elected by the qualified electors on the second Monday of September annually"—which motion passed in the affirmative, and the second section, as amended, passed, one hundred and thirty-seven members in the affirmative, ninety-five in the negative.

Mr. Herrick of Bowdoinham, then moved a reconsideration of the last vote; a debate ensued, which continued until the usual hour of adjournment, when the convention adjourned until 3 o'clock this afternoon.

AFTERNOON.

Met. The convention resumed the consideration of Mr. Herrick's motion, when the question was taken, and the motion for reconsideration prevailed, two hundred and seventeen members voting in favor of the reconsideration, and thirty-one against it.

On motion of Mr. Rose of Boothbay, *Ordered,* That the second section, as amended, and third section, fourth article, be now both taken into consideration, that the whole subject of representation may be considered at the same time.

Mr. Herrick of Bowdoinham, then submitted the following amendment: "Every town in this State, heretofore represented in the House of Representatives of Massachusetts, shall elect one representative;

Every other town in the State containing one thousand inhabitants shall elect one representative, and every town in this State containing three thousand inhabitants, shall elect two representatives, and for every additional three thousand inhabitants an additional representative: *Provided* no town shall be entitled to more than five representatives; and any two or more towns or plantations whose inhabitants shall not be sufficient to entitle each to a representative, but whose inhabitants together shall amount to one thousand, may voluntarily associate themselves together from year to year for that purpose, and shall be entitled to one representative."

The question on Mr. Herrick's amendment was taken up, and after much debate, the subject was postponed, and the convention

Adjourned until to-morrow morning at half-past 8 o'clock.

THURSDAY, October 21, 1819.

Met according to adjournment.

The Committee on Elections reported that Thomas A. Johnson, Esq., the delegate returned from the town of Cornish, in the county of York, has been duly certified, and he is in the opinion of the committee, entitled to his seat—which report was accepted.

Mr. Herrick's amendment was taken up, and after much debate, was withdrawn by the mover, and

Gen. Wingate of Bath submitted the following amendment: "The House of Representatives, first to be elected under this constitution, shall consist of members to be chosen by the several incorporated towns within this State, each town being entitled to the same number as though this constitution had not been adopted; *provided, however*, that all such towns and plantations as would not be entitled to a representative, may by a major vote and mutual agreement among themselves, class themselves for the purpose of electing a representative, and the representative so chosen by any class shall produce to the House of Representatives together with the proper evidence of their election, an attested copy of the vote of the several towns and plantations forming such a class, to class themselves for the purpose of such election, and also a certificate of the assessors of such towns and plantations, of the number of polls in their respective towns and plantations. The House of Representatives to be elected on the second Monday of September 1821, and forever thereafter, shall consist of not less than one hundred members nor more than two hundred, and shall continue in service one year from the day next preceeding the annual meeting of the Legislature; *Provided, however*, that until the population of the State shall amount to five hundred thousand, the number of representatives shall not exceed two hundred and fifty. And the Legislature shall, before the first day of May, 1821, and within every subsequent period of at most ten years, cause the number of inhabitants of the State, to be ascertained, exclusive of foreigners not naturalized and Indians not taxed—and the number of representatives shall at the several periods of making such enumeration be fixed and determined by the Legislature, which members so fixed and determined, shall first be apportioned by the Legislature, among the several counties in the State, as near as may be according to their number of inhabitants, having regard to the relative increase of population. And the Legislature shall further apportion the representatives, so assigned to the respective counties, among the towns in their respective counties, as near as may be on the principle of equality, giving to each individual town that may be entitled thereto, upon such ratio as shall be established by the Legislature, one or more members, and classing the towns and plantations not entitled to one member in such manner, that each class may elect one representative;" which motion was considered, and a debate ensued thereon, which continued until the usual hour of adjournment, when the convention adjourned to 3 o'clock P. M.

AFTERNOON.

Met. The convention resumed the consideration of General Wingate's amendment, when by consent of the mover, the amendment was permitted to lie upon the table—and the convention took again into consideration the second and third section of the fourth article.

Judge Bridge moved to strike out "two" and insert "three"—which motion was put and decided in the negative, fifty-two for the motion and one hundred and sixty against it.

Mr. Usher then moved to strike out "two hundred" in the second line, which was also negatived.

Hon. Mr. Whitman then moved further to amend by striking out the second section, and to insert in lieu thereof, the following: "For the purpose of electing representatives, each county shall be divided into districts, consisting of one or more entire towns, comprising contiguous territory, the exterior limits of each of which, if consisting of more than one town, shall be as nearly equally distant from a common centre as may be; and not exceeding or falling short more than two per centum of the precise number of inhabitants, requisite to entitle such district to send one representative. But whenever a district cannot be formed in manner aforesaid, consisting of more towns than one, comprising the number of inhabitants to entitle it to elect one representative, a district may be formed, in manner aforesaid, containing the requisite number—or within ten per centum more or less thereof, to entitle it to elect a greater number being as few as practicable; and in no case exceeding five representatives. *Provided, however*, that any single town, containing within ten per centum of more or less than the requisite number of inhabitants, to entitle it to elect one or more representatives, shall be considered as a district for the purpose of electing the corresponding number of representatives. The number of inhabitants in any county, entitled to a representative, shall be equivalent as near as may be, to the product of the whole number of inhabitants in such county, divided by the number of representatives assigned to it"—which motion was put and decided in the negative.

Judge Cony then moved further to amend the second line in second section, by striking out "two" and in lieu thereof to insert "one hundred and fifty"—which motion was also negatived, twenty-four members only voting in favor.

Hon. Mr. Holmes moved further to amend by inserting at the end of the second section the following: "and, whenever the number of representatives shall amount to two hundred, at the next annual meeting of elections, which shall thereafter happen at any subsequent period of ten years, the people shall give in their votes on the question whether the number of representatives shall be increased or diminished; and if a majority of the votes are in favor thereof, it shall be the duty of the next Legislature thereafter, to increase or diminish the number by the rule hereinafter prescribed"—which motion was passed in the affirmative, sixteen members only voting against the amendment.

The amendment proposed by Gen. Wingate was again taken into consideration, and motion was made to commit the same together with the several propositions which had been submitted relative to representation—which motion was negatived, and the question was then taken on the amendment offered which also passed in the negative.

The second section of the fourth article then passed—one hundred and ninety-one members voting in favor, and thirty-six against.

Voted to adjourn to half-past 8 o'clock.

Adjourned accordingly.

FRIDAY, October 22, 1819.

Met according to adjournment.

The convention took into consideration the third section, fourth article, of the constitution.

Col. Atherton moved to strike out the third section, and insert in lieu thereof the following: "The number of representatives shall be apportioned to the number of inhabitants of each county; the counties shall be divided into districts of three, six and nine thousand; and every such district shall be entitled to one representative for every three thousand inhabitants: *Provided, however*, that a district containing more than one town and entitled to more than one representative, shall not choose both of said representatives from one town." The question was put upon that part of the motion which relates to dividing the State into County districts for the choice of representatives—which motion was negatived, and the amendment did not prevail.

Hon. Mr. Holmes then moved to strike out, in the eleventh and twelfth lines, the following words: "*and provided further*, that the whole number of representatives shall never be more than two hundred"—which motion passed in the affirmative.

Mr. Allen of Norridgewock, moved further to amend the second section in the first line, by sriking out fifteen hundred and insert "twelve hundred"—which motion passed in the negative, eighty-six members voting in favor, and one hundred and fifty against it.

Mr. Herrick of Bowdoinham, moved further to amend the third section, by inserting in the seventh line, between the word "and," and the word "towns," "any two or more towns and plantations;" and, in the 8th line, by inserting after the word "inhabitants," "but whose inhabitants shall amount to that number, who may voluntarily unite from year to year for that purpose, shall be entitled to one representative"—which motion was also negatived.

Mr. Hobbs of Waterborough, moved to insert after the word towns, in the seventh line, the following amendment, "and plantations duly organized"—which motion passed in the affirmative.

Mr. Abbot of Castine, moved a further amendment in the thirteenth line, after the word "apportionment," by striking out, "it shall contain that number," and in lieu thereof, to insert, "the House of Representatives shall contain two hundred members"—which motion passed in the affirmative.

Mr. Emery moved a further amendment to strike out "three," and to insert "five" in the fourth line—which motion was negatived.

Mr. Parsons of Edgcomb, moved to insert at the end of the third section, "and any two towns having a sufficient number of inhabitants to elect one representative, shall be joined together, with the privilege of electing a representative alternately, beginning with the oldest town, or by an agreement of both towns may jointly elect one annually"—which motion was negatived, twenty-seven in the affirmative and one hundred and thirty-five in the negative. The third section of the fourth article passed; two hundred and three members voting in the affirmative, and forty-one in the negative.

Section fourth was then taken into consideration.

Hon. Mr. Holmes moved to amend by inserting after the word "elected," in the third line, these words, "a citizen of the United States for five years"—which motion prevailed.

Mr. Lock moved to strike out "one," and insert "five," in the fourth line—which motion was withdrawn by the mover, and renewed by Mr. Baldwin, and the question was put and decided in the negative, forty-six members voting in the affirmative, and one hundred and forty-four in the negative.

Mr. Virgin moved further to amend, by inserting after the word "resident," in the sixth line, these words, "for three months next preceding his election"—which motion passed in the affirmative.

The fourth section then passed as amended.

Section fifth was then considered.

Hon. Mr. Holmes moved to amend by striking out these words in the first and second lines of the fifth section: "The representatives shall be chosen by the qualified electors on the second Monday of September, annually;" and to insert after the word "meetings," these words, "for the choice of representatives"—which motion passed in the affirmative, without division.

Hon. Mr. Holmes moved further to amend in the thirty-second line of the same section, after the word "elected," and to insert the the following: "and the clerks of the towns and plantations respectively shall seal up copies of all such lists and cause them to be delivered into the Secretary's Office, twenty days, at least, before the first Wednesday of January annually"—which motion also passed in the affirmative.

Mr. Dane of Wells, moved to amend in the seventeenth line, by striking out "be held," and insert these words, "hold their meetings"—which motion passed in the affirmative.

Mr. Davis of Gouldsborough, then moved further to amend in the twenty-fifth line, by striking out "two," and inserting in lieu thereof, "four"—which motion also prevailed, and the section was so amended.

The question was then taken on the fifth section, and the same passed as amended.

The sixth, seventh, and eighth sections, were severally taken up and passed, and the Convention

Adjourned until 3 o'clock this afternoon.

AFTERNOON.

Met. Leave of absence was given to Mr. McCobb of Phipsburg, after this day.

Col. Moore of Clinton, presented the petition of James Gray and others, on the subject of the Militia—which was read and ordered to lie upon the table.

The first section of the fourth article, second part, was taken into consideration.

Judge Cony moved to amend in the first and second lines of the first section, by striking out the following: "of not less than twenty-three, nor more than thirty-one"—which motion was advocated by the Hon. mover, and passed in the negative.

The first section then passed without amendment.

Mr. Dearborn of Hallowell, gave notice that he should on Monday next, at 12 o'clock, move a reconsideration of the vote passed upon the second and third section of the fourth article, first part of the Constitution, relative to representation in the House of Representatives.

The second section was then considered.

Hon. Mr. Holmes then moved to amend said section in the ninth and tenth lines, by striking out "one for every increase of eight members," and inserting these words, "until it shall arrive at the number of thirty-one, according to the increase"—which motion passed in the affirmative.

Mr. Dearborn of Hallowell, moved to strike out in the eighth line the word "three," and insert "four"—which motion was negatived, and the second section passed as amended.

Sections third, fourth and fifth, were then severally considered, and passed without amendment.

The sixth section was then considered.

Hon. Mr. Holmes moved to amend, by inserting at the beginning of the sixth section, these words: "The Senators shall be twenty-five years of age, at the commencement of the term for which they are elected, and in all other respects their," and to strike out "The" and of "Senators," in the first line—which motion passed, and the sixth section passed as amended.

The seventh and eighth sections also passed.

Article fourth, part third, sections first, second, third, fourth, fifth and sixth, passed severally without amendment.

Section seventh was then taken into consideration, and the Hon. Mr. Holmes moved to strike out these words in the seventh section, commencing in the fourth line: "The expenses of the members of the House of Representatives, in traveling to the Legislature, and returning therefrom, once in every session, and no more, shall be paid by the State, out of the public treasury, to every member who shall seasonably attend, in the judgment of the House, and does not depart therefrom without leave." A debate ensued upon this amendment, which continued until the usual hour of adjournment.

Mr. Low of Lyman, and Mr. Morrill of Wells, asked and obtained leave of absence.

Voted to adjourn to half-past 8 o'clock to-morrow morning.

Adjourned accordingly.

SATURDAY, October 23, 1819.

Met according to adjournment.

Ordered, That the revising committee, to whom has been committed the preamble and first article of the constitution, be be authorized to cause the same to be engrossed.

Dr. Thayer of Fairfield, asked and obtained leave of absence after this day.

The convention resumed the consideration of the seventh section, fourth article, part third, of the constitution.

Hon. Mr. Holmes amendment was taken up and decided in the negative, thirty-eight members voting in the affirmative, and one hundred and fifty-six in the negative.

Rev. Mr. Hooper of Paris, moved to strike out these words: "The Senators and Representatives shall receive such compensation as shall be established by law," and to insert in lieu thereof, "The Senators and Represenatives shall receive ——— compensation for their services, which shall not be increased or diminished, to take effect during the term for which they are elected"—which motion was negatived.

Judge Greene then moved further to amend, by inserting at the end of the seventh section, these words: "but the attendance of the members shall be paid by the several towns and classes, in which they shall have been elected"—which motion was negatived.

Mr. Herrick of Bowdoinham, moved further to amend in the first line, between the words "receive" and "such," by inserting these words, "out of the treasury of the State," and to strike out what remains of the section after the period following the word "it," in the fourth line—which motion was also negatived.

Hon. Mr. Holmes then moved further to amend by inserting at the end of the section, these words: "and they shall be paid for their attendance out of the public treasury, and the expense thereof shall be assessed on the inhabitants of each county, according to their number of representatives"—which motion was negatived, twenty members voting in the affirmative, and one hundred and forty-seven in the negative.

The seventh section then passed without amendment.

Sections eighth, ninth and tenth, were severally read and paesed without amendment.

The eleventh section was then considered.

Mr. Vance moved to amend by striking out in the second line, "Post Offices"—which motion, after some debate, was withdrawn by the mover.

Judge Thatcher then moved to strike out the following words: "no member of Congress, nor persons holding any office under the United States"—which motion was negatived.

Mr. Dane of Wells, moved to amend in the third line, and to insert after "Justices of the Peace," these words, "of the Sessions"—which motion was negatived.

Sections eleventh and twelfth, passed without amendment.

Article fifth, part first, section first, passed.

Section second was then considered.

Hon. Mr. Holmes moved to amend in the second line by striking out, "on the second Monday of September annually"—which motion passed in the affirmative, as did the second section as amended.

Section third. Hon. Mr. Holmes moved to amend in the seventh line, by inserting after the word "January," these words, "then next," and in the thirteenth line, to insert after the word "list," these words, "if so many there be"—which motion passed in the affirmative, and the third section passed as amended.

Sections fifth, sixth and seventh, severally passed without amendment.

Section eighth. Hon. Mr. Holmes moved to amend in the third line by striking out the word "and," before the word "register," and inserting after the word "Probate," these words, "and Notaries Public, and all other civil and military officers, whose appointment is not by this Constitution, or shall not by law be otherwise prescribed"—which motion prevailed, and the section passed as amended.

Sections ninth, tenth, eleventh, twelfth and thirteenth, were severally read and passed without amendment..

Article fifth, part second, section first. Hon. Mr. Holmes moved to insert after the words "citizens of," in the second line, these words, "the United States and resident"—which motion passed in the affirmative.

Mr. Leighton of Shapleigh, moved further to amend, by striking out "seven," and to insert in lieu thereof, "five"—on this motion a debate ensued, which continued until the usual hour of adjournment, when the Convention

Adjourned until 3 o'clock in the afternoon.

AFTERNOON.

Met. Mr. Leighton's amendment was considered, the question taken and decided in the negative, seventy-four members voting in the affirmative, and one hundred and ten in the negative.

Section first then passed as amended, without division.

Section second. Mr. Baldwin moved to amend by striking out in the first, second and third lines, these words, "on the first Wednesday of January, by a joint ballot of the Senators and Representatives in Convention," and to insert in lieu thereof, "by the qualified electors on the second Monday of September"—which motion was negatived.

Mr. Dickinson then moved further to amend by striking out "appointment" in the fifth line, and to insert "Election;" and on motion of Mr. Wallingford, the section was further amended by inserting at the end thereof, these words, "and they shall be privileged from arrest, in the same manner as Senators and Representatives." The second section then passed as amended.

Section third, second line. Hon. Mr. Whitman moved to insert after the word "present," these words, "who may agree thereto"—which motion prevailed, and the section passed as amended.

Section fourth. Hon. Mr. Holmes moved to amend by striking out "Senate and House of Representatives," and to insert "Legislature;" and the Hon. Mr. Whitman moved to strike out the word "under," in the third line, and to insert the words "in the executive departments of"—which amendments passed, and the fourth section passed as amended.

Article fifth, part third, Secretary. Sections first, second, third and fourth, were severally read and passed without amendment.

Article fifth, part fourth, Treasurer. Sections first, second, third and fourth, passed severally without amendment.

Article sixth, Judicial powers. Sections first, second, third, fourth, fifth and sixth, were severally read and passed without amendment.

Article seventh, Military. Section first. Col. Currier moved to amend by inserting after the word "companies," these words, "the electors shall be twenty-one years of age"—which motion was negatived.

On motion of Judge Bridge,

Ordered, That a committee of nine be appointed to take into consideration the apportionment of Senators and Representatives for the first Legislature, and to report such facts as they may find in relation thereto; and whether justice requires that any alterations should take place in such apportionment.

The Hon. Judge Greene, Judge Parris, Dr. Rose of Boothbay, Mr. Getchell of Vassalboro', Mr. Virgin of Rumford, Col. Trescott of Lubec, Major Treat of Bangor, Col. Atherton of Prospect, and Mr. Collins of Anson, were appointed the said committee.

Ordered, That the second, third, fourth, fifth and sixth articles of the constitution, be committed to the revising committee, that the same may be examined by them; and that they be directed to cause the same to be engrossed.

Mr. Butterfield of North Hill, Mr. Wallingford of Wells, and Mr. Wood of Wiscasset, asked and obtained leave of absence.

Voted, That when the convention adjourn, it be until half-past 8 o'clock, on the morning of Monday next.

Adjourned accordingly.

MONDAY, OCTOBER 25, 1819.

Met according to adjournment.

A communication was received from the Secretary of the Commonwealth of Massachusetts, inclosing a list of the votes given in, in the several towns, within the District of Maine, upon the subject of the separation of said District; which was ordered to be placed upon the files.

Gen. Wingate moved to reconsider the vote which passed on Saturday, on the amendment proposed by the Hon Mr. Whitman, in the fifth article, part second, section fourth, third line, which was in these words; strike out the word "under," and insert the words, "in the Executive departments of"—which motion prevailed, and the amendment was lost.

The Hon. Mr. Holmes then moved to insert after the word "State," in the second line, the words, "or persons holding any executive office under the United States, or this State, notaries public excepted"—which motion was taken into consideration, and afterwards withdrawn by the Hon. mover.

The Hon. Mr. Holmes moved the following amendment at the end of the third section, article fourth, part first, in these words: "and whenever any town, not entitled to elect a representative, shall determine against a classification with any other town or plantation, the Legislature shall, at each apportionment of representatives, on the application of each town, authorize it to elect a representative for such portion of time, and at such periods as shall be equal to its proportion of representatives, and the right of representation so established, shall not be altered until the next general apportionment; the amendment was taken up and considered, and a motion was made to commit the same; the motion prevailed, and the same was committed to Mr. Dole of Alna, Mr. Wood of Lebanon, Mr. Leach of Raymond, Mr. Lamson of Wayne, Doctor Perkins of Weld, Col. Atherton of Prospect, Mr. Neal of Madison, Mr. Wilkins of Orrington, and Mr. Burgin of Eastport.

Gen. Wingate then submitted a further amendment to the third section aforesaid, which was read and ordered to lie upon the table.

Section one, article seventh, Military, was then again taken into consideration.

Gen. Wingate moved to amend by inserting after the word "votes," in the second line, the words, "the members"—which motion prevailed, and the section passed as amended.

Section second was then considered.

Gen. Wingate moved to amend in the first line, by striking out after the word "the," these words, "time and manner of convening the electors, collecting the votes and certifying to the Governor the officers elected," and to insert the words, "the manner of notifying the electors, conducting the elections, and of making the returns to the Governor of the officers elected"—which motion prevailed, and the section passed as amended.

Section third. Hon. Mr. Holmes moved to amend the third and fourth lines, by striking out these words, "and the commanders of forts and garrisons," and to insert after the words "Adjutant General," the words "and Quartermaster General: *Provided* the Adjutant General shall perform the duties of Quartermaster General until otherwise directed by law"—which motion prevailed, and the Hon. Mr. Holmes moved to amend, by inserting at the end of section third these words, "and all military officers shall be commissioned by the Governor"—which motion prevailed, and the section was so amended.

Col. Hobbs of Berwick, moved further to amend by striking out in the first and second lines, these words: "The Major Generals shall be chosen by the Senate and House of Representatives, each having a negative on the other," and to insert, "the Major Generals shall be chosen by the Brigadier Generals, and the field officers in their respective divisions"—which motion was decided in the negative.

Mr. Abbot of Castine, moved to strike out the word "and," and to insert the words "with advice of," in the first line—which amendment prevailed, and the third section then passed as amended.

Section fourth passed without amendment.

Col. Stevens presented the petition of Jeremiah Bailey and others, upon the subject of the militia—which was read and ordered to lie upon the table.

Section fifth was then considered.

Mr. Hall of Buckfield, moved to amend the same by striking out the whole of said section, and to insert in lieu thereof, the following: "The militia, who are by law obliged to bear arms, shall have a reasonable compensation for their services"—upon which amendment a debate ensued which continued until the usual hour of adjournment, when the convention

Adjourned until 3 o'clock in the afternoon.

AFTERNOON.

Met. Mr. Hall's amendment was again considered, and the motion was amended by the mover, so as the same should read as an amendment, to be inserted at the end of the section, which motion was decided in the negative; seventy-four members voting in the affirmative, and one hundred and twenty-seven in the negative, so the motion was lost.

Col. Atherton then moved further to amend, by striking out the whole of the fifth section, and to insert in lieu thereof these words: "Section fifth. "No person of the age of eighteen years, and under the age of forty-five years, shall be exempted from the performance of duty in the militia, excepting the Justices of the Supreme Judicial Court, Ministers of the Gospel, Officers of the Militia who have been superceded or honorably discharged, and such other persons as are or may be exempted by the laws of the United States, unless he shall pay an equivalent, which said equivalent shall be paid to such officers, as a fund for clothing and equipping the Militia, and apportioned in such manner as the Legislature of the State may direct"—which motion was negatived.

Mr. Francis of Leeds, moved a further amendment by striking out the whole of the section under consideration, and in lieu thereof, to insert the following: "Persons whose religious sentiments forbid their engaging in war, may be exempted from military duty; but no person except the Justices of the Supreme Judicial Court, shall be exempted by reason of holding or having held any civil office under the State, without paying an equivalent"—which motion was passed in the negative.

Gen. Chandler moved further to amend by inserting at the end of the section, these words, "And all persons borne on the rolls of any Company of militia, and doing military duty therein, shall be exempt from poll-tax, in the State and County taxes, during the time he shall so do military duty—which motion passed in the negative.

Hon. Mr. Holmes moved to amend by striking out in the second line, the word "shall," and to insert the word "may"—which motion prevailed, and the fifth section then passed as amended.

Mr. Bradbury of York, asked and obtained leave of absence.

Voted, That when the Convention adjourn, it be until 7 o'clock this evening.

Adjourned accordingly.

EVENING.

Met according to adjournment.

Article eighth, Literature, was taken into consideration.

Dr. Rose moved to amend in the tenth line, by inserting after the word "made," the words "by the Legislature,"—which motion passed in the affirmative.

Mr. Shepley of Saco, moved to amend by striking out these words, "the Governor and Council, shall have the power of revising and negativing the doings and government of such institution, in the selection of its officers and the management of its fund;" and to insert in lieu thereof, the following: "The Legislature of the State, shall have the right to grant any further powers to, or alter, limit, or restrain any of the powers vested in any such literary institution, as shall be judged necessary to promote the best interest thereof"—which motion prevailed, one hundred and fifty-one members voting in the affirmative, and eighteen in the negative.

Mr. Stockbridge of North Yarmouth, moved further to amend, by striking out the whole of the "Proviso" in said section, in order to insert a substitute, which he read in his place; the the question was put upon striking out, and decided in the negative; so the motion was lost, and the article passed as amended.

Article ninth, General Provisions.

Section first. The Hon. Mr. Holmes moved to amend in the seventh and eighth lines, by striking out the words "of this State," in the seventh line, and to insert the same in the eighth line, after the word "States;" and further to amend by inserting at the end of the section, these words, "and whenever the Governor or any Councilor, shall not be able to attend during the session of the Legislature, to take and subscribe said oaths or affirmations, such oaths or affirmations may be taken and subscribed in the recess of the Legislature, before any Justice of the Supreme Judicial Court"—which motion prevailed, and the section passed as amended.

Section second. Gen. Wingate moved to amend, by inserting in the fourth line, after "Adjutant General," the words, "Quartermaster General;" and the Hon. Mr. Holmes moved further to amend by striking out in the third line, "Solicitor General;" and in the fifth line, between the words "Sheriff and Clerk," insert "or," and strike out "or Clerk of any inferior Court"—which motion passed in the affirmative, and the second section passed as amended.

Sections third, fourth and fifth, were severally read and passed.

Section sixth. Hon. Mr. Holmes moved to amend by inserting, after the word "for," at the end of the first line, these words, "or which shall not otherwise be provided by law," and to insert at the end of the section, "but not exceeding five years"—which motion prevailed.

Mr. Knight of Falmouth, moved further to amend by adding to the section these words: "No person who denies the christian religion shall hold any office in the civil department of this State"—which motion was advocated by the mover, and passed in the negative; the sixth section then passed as amended, without division.

Col. Atherton, gave notice that he should at 3 o'clock to-morrow afternoon, call up the resolution submitted by him, some days since, relative to the location of the seat of government.

Ordered, That so much of the constitution as has been accepted by the convention, be committed to the revising committee; and that Mr. Kingsbury of Gardiner, and Judge Ames of Bath, be added to said committee.

Voted to adjourn to half-past 8 o'clock to-morrow morning. Adjourned accordingly.

TUESDAY, OCTOBER 26, 1819.

Met according to adjournment.

Mr. Thrasher of Cape Elizabeth, moved that a Committee be appointed to report to this Convention, all laws of Massachusetts, which are repugnant to the Constitution of Maine—which motion was read and ordered to lie upon the table.

Judge Cony submitted the following resolution, which was read and ordered to lie upon the table.

Resolved, That a Committee of ——— be appointed to procure a suitable public Seal, and also a proper device for the Arms of the State.

Judge Greene, Chairman of the Committee appointed to take into consideration the apportionment of Senators and Representatives for the first Legislature, made a report, and a statement of facts in relation thereto, which were submitted. The Committee find the whole number of Inhabitants according to the most correct estimate, which they have been able to make, to be as follows, viz:

In the County of	No. of Inhabitants.	Senators.	Fraction wanting.	Excess.
York,	50,291	4	10,765	
Cumberland,	56,043	4	5,013	
Lincoln,	59,148	4	1,918	
Kennebec,	54,992	3		9,200
Oxford,	33,336	2		2,808
Somerset,	30,790	2		262
Hancock,	34,276	2		3,748
Penobscot,	19,126	1		3,862
Washington,	13,076	1	2,188	

And the opinion of the Committee upon the foregoing facts, is, that should the number of Senators be increased to twenty-four, justice requires that four Senators should be appointed to Kennebec, that county having a fraction much larger than any other according to the apportionment, made by a former Committee.

The above report was read, and thereupon

Resolved, That one additional Senator be added, so that the whole number of Senators which may be elected be increased to twenty-four; that this additional Senator be placed to the county of Kennebec, and that the report be so far amended, as that the county of Kennebec may be entitled to send four Senators to the first Legislature—which resolve was read and passed.

Mr. Johnson of Belfast, then moved that one additional Senator be added to the county of Hancock—which motion was afterwards withdrawn by the mover, and

The Hon. Mr. Holmes then moved to reconsider the former votes assigning the number of Senators to be elected and returned to the first Legislature; and to adopt the following apportionment of Senators to be elected for the first Legislature: The counties of York, Cumberland, Lincoln and Kennebec, may elect three each; the counties of Hancock, Oxford and Somerset, may elect two each; the counties of Washington and Penobscot, may elect one each, making the whole number of Senators for the first Legislature twenty—which motion passed in the affirmative.

Hon. Mr. Holmes moved to amend the fourth article, part second, in section first, line second; and in section second, line eighth, by striking out the word "three"—which motion prevailed.

Mr. Kingsbury of Gardiner, moved to reconsider the last vote—which motion was negatived.

Article tenth was then considered.

Section first. Mr. Dane of Wells, moved to amend by inserting after the word "next," in the second line, these words: "The choice of Councilors, Secretary and Treasurer, on the first Wednesday of January annually, shall not be made until the year of our Lord, eighteen hundred and twenty-two;" and further to amend said section in the fourth line, by inserting after the word "time," these words: "The choice of Councilors, Secretary and Treasurer, shall be made on the last Wednesday of May next"—which motion passed in the affirmative.

Hon. Mr. Holmes moved further to amend by striking out the word "four," and to insert "three," in the twenty-fourth, twenty-fifth and twenty-sixth lines," which motion prevailed; and further to amend in the thirty-seventh line, by striking out "members," and to insert the word "numbers"—which passed in the affirmative.

On motion of Mr. Dearborn, the convention resolved themselves into a committee of the whole, upon the subject of representation in the House of Representatives; Hon. Judge Thatcher in the chair. After some time in committee, the Honorable President resumed the chair, and the Honorable Chairman reported: That the committee had, according to order, had the subject committed to them, under consideration; had made some progress, and asked leave to sit again; which report was stated from the Chair, and thereupon

Resolved, That the committee of the whole convention, have leave to sit again.

Mr. Burnham of Limerick, asked and obtained leave of absence.

Adjourned to 3 o'clock this afternoon.

AFTERNOON.

Met. The convention again resolved themselves into a committe of the whole, and, after sometime spent therein, the Honorable President resumed the chair, and the Hon. Judge Thatcher reported that the committee of the whole convention, had had under consideration the subject of representation in the House of Representatives; had made some progress, and asked leave to sit again, and thereupon

Resolved, That the said committee have leave to sit again.

Voted, That when the convention adjourn, it be until 7 o'clock this evening.

Adjourned accordingly.

EVENING.

Met. The convention again resolved themselves into a committee of the whole, upon the subject of representation in the House of Representatives, and after some time spent therein, the Honorable President resumed the chair, and the Hon. Judge Thatcher reported, that the committee of the whole convention had had under consideration the second and third sections of the fourth article of the constitution, relative to representation in the House of Representatives, and directed him to report the same, without amendment; which report was accepted.

Voted, That when the convention adjourn, it be until half-past 8 o'clock to-morrow morning.

Adjourned accordingly.

WEDNESDAY, October 27, 1819.

Met according to adjournment.

Hon. Mr. Holmes, chairman of the revising committee, reported the second, third and fourth articles of the constitution, as examined by them, and thereupon

Ordered, That the said articles now be engrossed.

The Preamble and Bill of Rights, or first article of the constitution, as reported by the revising committee, as being correctly engrossed, was again read, and the same passed unanimously.

On motion of the Hon Mr. Moody,

To-morrow, at 10 o'clock, was assigned for coming to the choice of a Secretary of State *pro tempore,* and that nominations be suspended in the meantime.

Resolved, That Mr. Preble of Cumberland, Mr. Thatcher, junior, of York, Judge Ames of Lincoln, Mr. Jarvis of Hancock, Mr. Burgin of Washington, Mr. Gage of Kennebec, Mr. Virgin of Oxford, Mr. Coburn of Somerset, and Mr. Stetson of Penobscot, be a committee to prepare an address, in behalf of this convention, to the people of Maine, to be distributed with the constitution submitted to the people.

Mr. Boyd of Limington, asked and obtained leave of absence.

The convention further considered the motion made by Mr. Dearborn, for reconsideration of the vote relative to the subject of representation in the House of Representatives; and the motion was so far withdrawn by the mover, as to admit the following:

The Hon. Mr. Holmes moved to amend the third section, fourth article, in the second line: strike out "four thousand," and insert "three thousand seven hundred and fifty;" and in the fourth line, strike out "seven thousand five hundred," and insert "six thousand seven hundred and fifty"—which motion passed in the affirmative.

A further amendment was then moved by the Hon. Mr. Holmes, by inserting at the end of the third section, fourth article, part first, these words: "And whenever any town or towns, plantation or plantations, not entitled to elect a representative, shall determine against a classification with any other town or plantation, the Legislature may, at each apportionment of representatives, on the application of such town or plantation, authorize it to elect a representative for such portion of time and such period as shall be equal to its portion of representation, and the right of representation, so established, shall not be altered, until the next general apportionment"—which amendment passed in the affirmative, and the said sections were so amended.

Several propositions were made in writing, as substitutes for the second and third sections, fourth article of the Constitution; these propositions were from Mr. Wilson of Bingham, Mr. Stevens of China, Mr. Baldwin of Mercer, Mr. Grover of Bethel, Mr. Neal of Elliot, Mr. Tucker of Standish, Mr. Thomas of Eden, Major Swan of Winslow, Mr. Allen of Norridgewock, Mr. Shaw of Newport, Dr. Rose of Boothbay, Judge Cony of Augusta, Major Treat of Bangor, Mr. Riley of Newry, Mr. Leonard of Brewer, and Mr. Johnson of Jackson—which were severally read, and ordered to be placed upon the files of the Convention.

Article eleventh, Section first, was again taken into consideration.

—— —— moved to amend by striking out the arrangement made as in the printed report for the county of Penobscot, and to insert in lieu thereof, the following: "The towns of Hampden and Newburg may elect one representative; Orrington and Brewer, Eddington and Plantation adjacent on the east side Penobscot, one; Bangor, Orono, and Sunkhase Plantation, one; Dixmont, Newport, Carmel, Hermon, Stetson and Plantation No. 4, in the 6th Range, one; Levant, Corinth, Exeter, New Charleston, Blakesburg, Plantation No. 1, in the 3d Range, and Plantation No. 1, in the 4th Range, one; Dexter, Garland, Guilford, Sangerville, and Plantation No. 3, in the 6th Range, one; Atkinson, Sebec, Foxcroft, Brownville, Williamsburgh, Plantation No. 1, 7th Range, and No. 3, in 7th Range, one"—which motion prevailed.

And the section was further amended by inserting the following arrangement and apportionment for the county of Oxford: "The towns of Dixfield, Mexico, Weld, and Plantations Nos. 1 and 4, one representative; Jay and Hartford, one; Livermore, one; Rumford, East Andover, and Plantations Nos. 7 and 8, one; Turner, one; Woodstock, Paris, and Greenwood, one; Hebron and Norway, one; Gilead, Bethel, Newry, Albany, and Howard's Gore, one; Porter, Hiram and Brownfield, one; Waterford, Sweden and Lovel, one; Denmark, Fryeburg and Fryeburg addition, one; Buckfield and Turner, one.

The apportionment of Representatives for the counties of Lincoln and Hancock, were committed to the delegates from said counties, respectively, for them to consider said appointment, and to report this afternoon.

Section second, line second. Mr. Kingsbury moved to amend by striking out the word "are," and to insert these words, "first elected and appointed"—which motion prevailed, and the section passed as amended.

Sections third and fourth passed without amendment.

Section fourth. Col. Moody moved to amend in the ninth line by striking out these words, "or shall not"—which motion prevailed, and the section passed as amended.

Sections fifth and sixth passed without amendment.

Adjourned to 3 o'clock this afternoon.

AFTERNOON.

Met. *Resolved,* That Col. Moody, Judge Parris, Gen. Chandler, Gen. Kendall, and Col. Pond, be a committee to consider and report the day to be named by the convention, when the inhabitants of the several towns and plantations shall give in their votes for, or against the adoption of the constitution for the new State; and also the manner in which the constitution shall be published and distributed together with the accompanying address.

The committee composed of the delegates from the County of Lincoln, made a report upon the subject of the apportionment of representatives in said county, to amend in the third line after "Putnam," insert "Patricktown Plantation," and in the fifth line to strike out "Nobleborough and Newcastle," and to insert "Woolwich and Dresden"—which report was read and accepted.

The committee of delegates for the County of Hancock, made a report as follows: Strike out after the word "one," in the sixth line to the end of the paragraph, and to insert the following: "Lincolnville, Searsmont and Belmont, one representative; Belfast and Northport, one; Prospect and Swanville, one; Frankfort and Monroe, one; Knox, Brooks, Jackson and Thorndike, one"—which report was read and accepted.

The following amendment was offered by Col. Lewis, to be added to Article ninth—General Provisions:

"Section seventh. And while the public charges of the State or any part thereof, shall be assessed on polls or estates, in the manner that has hitherto been practised, in order that such assessments may be made with equality, there shall be a valuation of estates, within the State, taken anew, once in every ten years at least, and as much oftener as the Legislature shall direct"—the above amendment passed in the affirmative, without division.

Col. Atherton moved to reconsider the vote relative to the fifth section, seventh article of the constitution, passed the 25th instant, and is in these words: "Section fifth. Persons of the denomination of Quakers and Shakers may be exempt from military duty, but no person except the Justices of the Supreme Judicial Court, shall be exempted by reason of holding, or having held, any civil office under this State, without paying an equivalent"—the motion for reconsideration prevailed, and the section was striken out; and, on motion of Col. Atherton, the following substitute was adopted:

"Section fifth. Persons of the denomination of Quakers and

Shakers, Justices of the Supreme Judicial Court, ordained and settled ministers of the Gospel, may be exempted from military duty; but no other person of the age of eighteen, and under the age of forty-five years, excepting officers of the militia, who have been honorably discharged, shall be so exempted, unless he shall pay an equivalent, to be fixed by law "—which motion prevailed, and the section was so amended.

Several amendments were proposed to the constitution and negatived.

Mr. Thomas of Friendship, asked and obtained leave of absence, after this day.

Voted to adjourn to half-past 8 o'clock to-morrow morning. Adjourned accordingly.

THURSDAY, OCTOBER 28, 1819.

Met according to adjournment.

Mr. Weymouth of Belmont, submitted a proposition relative to the Judiciary, which was read and ordered to lie upon the table.

Ordered, That Col. Moody, Judge Parris, Gen. Chandler, Gen. Kendall, and Col. Pond, be a committee to consider and report the time and place to which this Convention shall adjourn, in order that they may finish the business assigned them, by an act relating to the separation of Maine from Massachusetts proper, and forming the same into a separate and independent State.

The Hon. Mr. Holmes moved the following amendment to be inserted in Article tenth—Schedule—Section first: "and in case of death or other disqualification of the President of this Convention, or of the Secretary of State *pro tempore,* before the election and qualification of the Governor or Secretary of State, under this Constitution, the persons to be designated by this Convention at their session in January next, shall have all the powers and perform all the duties, which the President of this Convention or the Secretary of State *pro tempore,* to be by them appointed, shall have and perform"—which amendment passed in the affirmative.

Hon. Mr. Moody, chairman of the committee appointed yesterday, upon the subject of printing and distributing the Constitution and address, submitted the following resolution, which was read and passed:

Resolved, That the Secretary of the Convention be authorized and required, to procure to be printed a sufficient number of copies of the Constitution and the address to the people of Maine, and distribute as soon as may be, one copy to the Selectmen of each town, and the Assessors of each district or plantation, one to each Clerk of the several towns and plantations, and one to each of the members of the Convention; and, also to cause the same to be published in the several newspapers printed within this district.

The same Committee reported the following resolution:

Resolved, That when the business of the first session of this Convention is completed, the Convention will adjourn to meet on the first Wednesday of January next, at the Court House in Portland—read and accepted.

Col. Atherton of Prospect, moved the following resolution, as a substitute for the one he had previously offered on the subject of location of the Seat of Goverment:

Resolved, That the first meeting of the Legislature of the State of Maine, and for the organization of its Government, shall be in the town of Portland; which was read, and ordered that the above resolution be committed to the committee appointed to prepare and report a Constitution or frame of Government for the new State.

On motion of Col. Moody, 3 o'clock this afternoon, was assigned for coming to the choice of a Treasurer.

Judge Campbell of Harrington, Mr. Vose of Robbinston, Mr. Allen of Norridgewock, Mr. Stockbridge of North Yarmouth, and the Rev. Mr. Hooper of Paris, asked and obtained leave of absence.

Agreeably to assignment, the Convention proceeded to the choice of a Secretary of State *pro tempore.*

Mr. Preble of Portland, Judge Greene, Gen. Chandler, Mr. Dole of Alna, and Mr. Johnson of Belfast, were appointed a committee to collect, sort and count the votes, for a Secretary of State *pro tempore*, for the new State.

The Committee reported that the whole number of votes given in, were two hundred and seventy-seven; necessary to a choice, one hundred and thirty-nine; no person having that number, the Convention proceeded to a second ballot; when it appeared that the whole number of votes was two hundred and ninety; necessary to a choice, one hundred and forty-six; Ashur Ware, Esq., had one hundred and fifty-seven votes, and was declared elected.

Resolved, That Judge Parris, Hon. Mr. Whitman, and Mr. Preble, be a committee to receive the returns of the several towns and plantations, approving or disapproving of the Constitution prepared by this Convention—read and accepted.

Ordered, That the committee on the pay roll, be requested to make up the roll, including to-morrow.

Articles second, third, fourth, fifth, sixth, seventh and eighth, of the constitution, were reported by the revising committee, as having been examined by them as correctly engrossed, were severally read and passed.

Adjourned to 3 o'clock this afternoon.

AFTERNOON.

Met. Mr. Low of Lyman, submitted the following resolution:

Resolved, unanimously, That this convention present their thanks to their Honorable President, for the candor and impartiality, with which he has conducted in his office, and for his successful endeavors to preserve peace and harmony during our session; and that we tender him our wish for a happy return to his family, and the possession of all those blessings which sensibility can enjoy.

Which resolve was read by the Secretary and unanimously adopted.

Upon which the Honorable President made the following reply:

" *Gentlemen of the Convention:*

This testimony of your approbation is to me invaluable. If I have been successful in the discharge of the duties which the partiality of friends assigned me, to your uniform candor and support it must be attributed; which will always be gratefully acknowledged.

" Permit me, gentlemen, to congratulate you upon the harmony and mutual respect which has prevailed during your deliberations, and to hope that this spirit of toleration and good will, will be generaly diffused by your example.

"I will only add, my best wishes for your prosperity and happiness, and that for your public services, as well as your individual exertions, you may receive the confidence and gratitude of your fellow citizens."

Agreeably to assignment, the convention proceeded to the choice of a Treasurer.

Mr. Preble of Portland, Judge Greene, Gen. Chandler, Mr. Dole of Alna, and Mr. Johnson of Belfast, were appointed a committee to collect, sort and count the votes for a Treasurer; when it appeared that the

Whole number of votes given in, was .	263
Necessary to a choice, . . .	132
And Hon. Albion K. Parris had . .	222

votes, and he was declared elected.

Mr. Wilkins of New Charleston, moved the following amendment to the tenth article of the constitution, in these words: "Section eighth. All taxes upon real estate, assessed by the authority of this State, shall be apportioned and assessed equally, according to the just value thereof"—which motion passed in the affirmative, and the section passed as engrossed.

The remaining articles of the constitution were reported by the revising committee, as being correctly engrossed, and the same were severally read and passed:

And the question was put upon the acceptance of the constitution for the new State, as reported by the committee, and now engrossed as amended, and the same passed in the affirmative; two hundred and thirty-six members voting in the affirmative, and thirty in the negative.

Mr. Coburn of Bloomfield, Mr. Sprague of Avon, Mr. Legrow of Lebanon, Mr. Adams of Gorham, Messrs. Cutler and Gay of Farmington, Mr. Lamson of Wayne, Mr. Francis of Leeds, Mr. Abbot of Castine, Mr. French of St. Albans, Mr. Herrick of Bowdoinham, and Mr. Waugh of Starks, asked and obtained leave of absence.

Voted to adjourn to half-past 8 o'clock to-morrow morning.

Adjourned accordingly.

FRIDAY, OCTOBER 29, 1819.

Met according to adjournment.

Gen. Wingate submitted the following resolutions:

Resolved, That the thanks of this convention be presented to the Reverend Clergymen, who have performed religious exercises during our session, for the able, devout and satisfactory manner in which they have discharged their duty.

Resolved, That the thanks of this convention be presented to the members of the First Parish in Portland, for the use of the meeting-house of said Parish, gratuitously and generously furnished by them for the accommodation of this convention.

The above resolutions were unanimously adopted.

Ordered, That the Secretary of this convention be directed to notify the Hon. Albion K. Parris, that he has been elected by the convention their Treasurer; and also that he notify Ashur Ware, Esquire, that he has been elected by this convention, Secretary *pro tempore,* of the State of Maine.

Resolved, That the constitution adopted by this convention, be published and sent to the several towns, districts and plantations, within the District of Maine; and, that the inhabitants thereof qualified by law be required to assemble in their respective towns, districts and plantations, on the first Monday of December next, to give in their votes in writing, expressing their approbation or disapprobation of said constitution—read and accepted.

Resolved, That the Secretary of State *pro tempore,* and the Secretary of this convention, be directed to superintend the printing of the constitution; and, also the several resolves which have been passed by this convention, and ordered to be published—read and accepted.

Resolved, That the Treasurer of the convention be authorized to borrow such sum of money, as may be necessary to pay the members of this convention—read and accepted.

Resolved, That the Secretary of State *pro tempore,* be requested to procure from the office of the Secretary of State of the United States, authenticated copies of the reports of the several Boards of Commissioners, relative to the boundaries and limits of the State of Maine, in that department; and, likewise, authenticated copies of all grants, and confirmation of grants, relative to the title and boundaries of the said State, in the office of the Secretary of State of the Commonwealth of Massachusetts; and that they be placed in the office of the Secretary of State of this State—read and accepted.

Resolved, That the application to Congress for the admission of the State of Maine into the Union, be signed by the President, and forwarded to Congress by the Senators and the Representatives in Congress from Maine—read and accepted.

Resolved, That Judge Parris, Mr. Preble, and the Hon. Mr. Whitman, be a committee to prepare a proper form of a return of votes on the question of the acceptance of the constitution, to be forwarded to the selectmen of the several towns, and assessors of the several plantations—read and accepted.

The committee to whom had been committed the subject of the location of the seat of government, and to designate the place where the first meeting of the Legislature shall be held, reported, that they had attended to the duty assigned them, and submitted the following resolution, as taken into a new draft:

Resolved, That Portland be the place for the first meeting of the Legislature for the State of Maine—which resolve was read and accepted, one hundred and seventy-five members voting in the affirmative, and seventy in the negative.

Resolved, That the constitution, as accepted by this convention, be signed by the President, and countersigned by the Secretary; and that the Secretary cause the names of those members who have signed the constitution to be entered on the journal, and that the same be annexed to, and printed with the constitution—read and accepted.

A communication was received from Ashur Ware, Esq., signifying his acceptance of the office of Secretary *pro tempore*, which was read.

The committee on the expenses of the convention exclusive of the pay roll, made a report, which was read, and

Ordered, That the Treasurer be requested to pay to the several persons mentioned in said report, the sums set against their names respectively; amounting in the whole, to the sum of five hundred twelve dollars and twenty-nine cents.

Adjourned to 3 o'clock this afternoon.

AFTEROON.

Met. *Ordered*, That the Treasurer be directed to pay John Merrick, Esq., of Hallowell, the sum of twenty dollars, for services by him rendered, as by his account, examined and allowed.

On motion of the Hon. President,

Resolved, unanimously, That the thanks of this convention be presented to the committee appointed to prepare and report a constitution or frame of government for the new State, for the ability and unwearied attention bestowed upon the subject committed to them.

The committee on the pay roll, made a report, by which it appeared that the travel and attendance of the members of this convention amounts to the sum of ——, which was accepted, and *Ordered*, That the Treasurer be directed to pay the same.

Resolved, That an additional number of copies of the constitution be printed, in order that the selectmen, town clerks and delegates, be furnished with four copies each instead of one copy each, as before provided.

Agreeably to the resolution offered in the morning, the Constitution was signed by the Hon. President, countersigned by the Secretary, and subscribed by the members, in the following manner.

Done in Convention October 29, 1819.

WILLIAM KING, *President of the Convention,*
and Member from Bath.

ROBERT C. VOSE, *Secretary.*

YORK COUNTY.

York, ...	Elihu Bragdon.
do	David Wilcox.
Kittery, . . .	Alexander Rice.
Berwick, . . .	William Hobbs.
do.	Nathaniel Hobbs.
do.	Richard F. Cutts.
Wells, ...	Joseph Thomas.
Arundel, . . .	Simon Nowell.
Parsonsfield, . . .	David Marston.
do.	Abner Keazer.
Saco, ...	Wm. Moody.
do.	Ether Shepley.
do.	Geo. Thatcher, Jr.
Lebanon, . . .	David Legrow.
Buxton, . . .	Gideon Elden.
do.	Josiah Paine.
do.	Edmund Woodman.
Lyman, . . .	John Low.
do.	John Burbank.
Biddeford, . . .	George Thatcher.
do.	Seth Spring.
Waterboro' . . .	Samuel Bradeen.
do.	Henry Hobbs.
Limington, . . .	David Boyd.
Cornish, . . .	Thomas A. Johnson.
Alfred, ...	John Holmes.
Hollis, ...	Ellis B. Usher.
do.	Timothy Hodgdon.
South Berwick, . .	Benj. Greene.
Limerick, . . .	John Burnham.
Shapleigh, . . .	John Leighton.

CUMBERLAND COUNTY.

Scarboro' . . .	Benjamin Larrabee, Jr.
do.	Joseph Fogg.
North Yarmouth, . .	William Buxton.
do.	Ephraim Sturdivant.
do.	Jeremiah Buxton.
Falmouth, . . .	Peter M. Knight.
do.	Nathan Buckman.
Standish, . . .	Theodore Mussey.

CUMBERLAND COUNTY, (Continued.)

Portland, . . .	Albion K. Parris.
do.	Wm. P. Preble.
Freeport, . . .	Solomon Dennison.
Durham, . . .	Secomb Jordan.
do.	Allen H. Cobb.
Bridgton, . . .	Phinehas Ingalls.
Poland, . . .	Josiah Dunn, Jr.
Brunswick, . . .	Robert D. Dunning.
do.	Jonathan Page.
do.	Benjamin Titcomb.
Harpswell, . . .	Stephen Purrington.
Gorham, . . .	Lathrop Lewis.
do.	Joseph Adams.
do.	James Irish.
Cape Elizabeth, . .	Ebenezer Thrasher.
New Gloucester, . .	Joseph E. Foxcroft.
do.	Isaac Gross.
Gray, ...	Joseph McLellan.
Minot, ...	Asaph Howard.
do.	Chandler Freeman.
Danville, . . .	Joseph Roberts.
Baldwin, . . .	Lot Davis.
Raymond, . . .	Zachariah Leach.
Pownal, . . .	Isaac Cushman.
Westbrook, ...	Silas Estes.
do.	Thomas Slemons.
do.	John Jones.
Harrison, . . .	Amos Thomas.

LINCOLN COUNTY.

Georgetown, . . .	Benjamin Riggs.
New Castle, . . .	Ebenezer Farley.
Woolwich, . . .	Ebenezer Delano.
Topsham, . . .	Nathaniel Greene.
Boothbay, . . .	Daniel Rose.
do.	John McKown.
Bristol, . . .	Samuel Tucker.
do.	Wm. McClintock.
do.	John Fossett.
Waldoboro' . . .	Joshua Head.
do.	Isaac G. Reed.

LINCOLN COUNTY, (Continued.)

Waldoboro', . . .	Jacob Ludwig, Jr.
Wiscasset, . . .	Abial Wood.
do.	Warren Rice.
Bowdoinham, . . .	Ebenezer Herrick.
do.	Elihu Hatch.
Nobleboro', . . .	Ephraim Rollins.
Cushing, . . .	Edward Killeran.
Camden, . . .	Nathaniel Martin.
Dresden, . . .	Isaac Lilley.
Lewiston, . . .	John Herrick.
Litchfield, . . .	John Neal.
do.	David C. Burr.
Lisbon, ...	Nathaniel Eames.
do.	James Small.
Edgcomb, . . .	Stephen Parsons.
Warren, . . .	John Miller.
do.	Cyrus Eaton.
Thomaston, . . .	Isaac Barnard.
do.	John Spear.
Bath, ...	Joshua Wingate, Jr.
do.	Benjamin Ames.
Union, ...	Robert Foster.
Bowdoin, . . .	Joseph Carr.
St. George, . . .	Joel Miller.
Hope, ...	Furgus McClaine.
Palermo, . . .	Thomas Eastman.
Montville, . . .	Cyrus Davis.
Jefferson, . . .	Jesse Rowell.
Friendship, . . .	Melzer Thomas.
Whitefield, . . .	Joseph Bailey.
Putnam, . . .	Mark Hatch.
Alna, ...	John Dole.
Wales, ...	Joseph Small.

KENNEBEC COUNTY.

Hallowell, . . .	Samuel Moody.
do.	Wm. H. Page.
do.	Benj. Dearborn.
Winthrop, . . .	Alexander Belcher.
do.	Daniel Campbell.
Vassalboro', . . .	Sam'l. Redington.

KENNEBEC COUNTY, (Continued.)

Vassalboro', . . .	Abiel Getchell.
Winslow, . . .	William Swan.
Pittston, . . .	Eli Young.
Greene, . . .	Luther Robbins.
Readfield, . . .	John Hubbard.
do.	Samuel Currier.
Sidney, . . .	Reuel Howard.
do. . . .	Ambrose Howard.
Farmington, . . .	Nathan Cutler.
do.	Jabez Gay.
New Sharon, . . .	Christopher Dyer.
Clinton, . . .	Herbert Moore.
Fayette, . . .	Charles Smith.
Belgrade, . . .	Elias Taylor.
Harlem, . . .	William Pullen.
Augusta, . . .	Daniel Cony.
do.	Joshua Gage.
do.	James Bridge.
Wayne, . . .	Joseph Lamson.
Monmouth, . . .	John Chandler.
do.	Simon Dearborn, Jr.
Mt. Vernon, . . .	David McGaffy.
Gardiner, . . .	Jacob Davis.
do.	Sanford Kingsbury,
Temple, . . .	Benjamin Abbot.
Wilton, . . .	Ebenezer Eaton.
Rome, ...	John S. Colbath.
Leeds, ...	Thomas Frances.
Chesterville, . . .	Ward Locke.
Vienna, . . .	Nathaniel Whittier.
Waterville, . . .	Abijah Smith.
do.	Ebenezer Bacon.
Fairfax, . . .	Joel Wellington.
Unity, ...	Rufus Burnham.
Malta, ...	William Hilton.
Freedom, . . .	Matthew Randall.
Joy, ...	James Parker.
China, ...	Daniel Stevens.

HANCOCK COUNTY.

Belfast, . . .	Alfred Johnson, Jr.
Isleboro', . . .	Josiah Farrow.
Deer Isle, . . .	Ignatus Haskell.
do.	Asa Green.
Bluehill, . . .	Andrew Witham.
Trenton, . . .	Peter Haynes.
Sullivan, . . .	George Henman.
Gouldsborough, . .	Samuel Davis.
Vinalhaven, . . .	Benj. Beverage.
Frankfort, . . .	Alexander Milliken.
do.	Joshua Hall.
Bucksport, . . .	Samuel Little.
Northport, . . .	David Alden.
Eden, ...	Nicholas Thomas, Jr.
Orland, . . .	Horatio Mason.
Ellsworth, . . .	Mark Shepard.
Lincolnville, . . .	Sam'l. A. Whitney.
Belmont, . . .	James Weymouth.
Brooks, . . .	Samuel Whitney.
Jackson, . . .	Boardman Johnson.
Searsmont, . . .	Ansel Lathrop.
Swanville, . . .	Eleazer Nickerson.
Thorndike, . . .	Joseph Blethen.
Monroe, . . .	Joseph Neally.
Prospect, . . .	Abel W. Atherton.
Castine, . . .	William Abbot.
Knox, ...	James Weed.

WASHINGTON COUNTY.

Machias, . . .	John Dickinson.
Steuben, . . .	Alexander Nichols.
Harrington, . . .	James Campbell.
Eastport, . . .	John Burgin.
Jonesborough, . . .	Ephraim Whitney.
Calais, ...	William Vance.
Lubec, ...	Lemuel Trescott.
Robbinston, . . .	Thomas Vose.
Cherryfield, . . .	Joseph Adams.
Perry, ...	Peter Golding.

OXFORD COUNTY.

Fryeburg, . . .	Judah Dana.
Turner, . . .	John Turner.
do.	Philip Bradford.
Hebron, . . .	Alexander Greenwood.
Buckfield, . . .	Enoch Hall.
Paris, ...	James Hooper.
do.	Benj. Chandler.
Norway, . . .	Aaron Wilkins.
Hartford, . . .	Joseph Tobin.
Sumner, . . .	Calvin Bisbee.
Rumford, . . .	Peter C. Virgin.
Lovell, ...	Josiah Heald, 2d.
Brownfield, . . .	James Steele.
Jay, ...	Cornelius Holland.
Livermore, . . .	Benjamin Bradford.
do.	Thomas Chase, Jr.
Bethel, ...	John Grover.
Waterford, . . .	Josiah Shaw.
Albany, . . .	Asa Cummings.
Dixfield, . . .	Solomon Leland.
East Andover, . . .	Sylvanus Poor.
Gilead, . . .	Eliphaz Chapman.
Newry, ...	Luke Reily.
Denmark, . . .	Cyrus Ingalls.
Porter, ...	William Towle.
Hiram, ...	Marshal Spring.
Woodstock, . . .	Cornelius Perkins.
Sweden, . . .	Samuel Nevers.
Mexico, . . .	Water P. Carpenter.
Greenwood, . . .	Isaac Flint.
Weld, ...	Lafayette Perkins.

SOMERSET COUNTY.

Canaan, . . .	Wentworth Tuttle.
Fairfield, . . .	William Kendall.
Norridgewock, . . .	William Allen, Jr.
Starks, . . .	James Waugh.
Cornville, . . .	George Bixby.
Anson, ...	James Collins.
Strong, ...	James Mayhew.

SOMERSET COUNTY, (Continued.)

Avon, ...	Samuel Sprague.
New Vineyard, . . .	William Talcott.
Harmony, . . .	Robert Evans.
Industry, . . .	Ezekiel Hinkley.
Athens, . . .	Isaiah Door.
Madison, . . .	John Neal.
Embden, . . .	Andrew McFadden.
Palmyra, . . .	Samuel Lancy.
Freeman, . . .	Jonathan Brown.
New Portland, . . .	Henry Norton.
Solon, ...	Elisha Coolidge.
Bingham, . . .	Obed Wilson.
Phillips, . . .	Joseph Dyer.
St. Albans, . . .	Benjamin French.
Kingfield, . . .	Joseph Knapp.
Corinna, . . .	William Elder.
Ripley, ...	Jacob Hale.
Bloomfield, . . .	Eleazer Coburn.
Warsaw, . . .	Stevens Kendall.

PENOBSCOT COUNTY.

Hampden, . . .	Simeon Stetson.
Orrington, . . .	John Wilkins.
Bangor, . . .	Joseph Treat.
Orono, . . .	Jackson Davis.
Dixmont, . . .	Samuel Butman.
New Charleston, . .	Daniel Wilkins.
Foxcroft, . . .	Samuel Chamberlain.
Sebec, ...	William Lowney.
Hermon, . . .	William Patten.
Levant, . . .	Moses Hodsden.
Brewer, . . .	Geo. Leonard.
Eddington, . . .	Luther Eaton.
Carmel, . . .	Abel Ruggles.
Corinth, . . .	Andrew Strong.
Exeter, . . .	Nathaniel Atkins.
Garland, . . .	Amos Gordon.
Newport, . . .	Benj. Shaw.
Sangerville, . . .	Benj. C. Goss.
Dexter, . . .	Isaac Farrar.

PENOBSCOT COUNTY, (CONTINUED.)

Guilford, . . .	Joseph Kelsey.
Atkinson, . . .	Eleazer W. Snow.
Newburgh, . . .	John Whitney.

Voted, That when the Convention adjourn, it be to meet at the Court House, in Portland, on the first Wednesday of January next, at 11 o'clock in the forenoon.

Adjourned accordingly.

ATTEST:—ROBERT C. VOSE, *Secretary.*

ADDRESS.

The Committee appointed on the 27th of October, 1819, to to prepare an address to the people of Maine, to accompany the Constitution to be submitted, made the following report, by Mr. PREBLE, their Chairman, which was printed by the previous order of the Convention. The following is the address:

To the People of Maine.

FELLOW CITIZENS:—The Delegates, elected to form a Constitution and Frame of Government, now present you the result of their deliberations.

They invite you to review it carefully, to weigh well its provisions. It is not submitted as a perfect system. In some few important provisions it is a compromise of conflicting interests and opinions; and, though not perfect, it is the best, upon which the convention under existing circumstances could agree.

In deciding upon its merits and demerits, the convention feel assured, you will be influenced by that candor and liberality, which always pervades an enlightened community.

The Constitution of Massachusetts, venerable as the work of the fathers of the revolution, endeared to the people by many associations and replete with the soundest principles of liberty and government, has in forty years experience proved inconvenient and defective in some few of its provisions.

Assuming that instrument for a basis, the convention proceeded to frame a Constitution for the State of Maine, deviating in those cases only, where the experience of this and of other States in the Union seemed to justify and require it.

They have omitted, as inconsistent with the dignity of the subject and the simplicity of "the truth," a provision, which, though *professing much*, is utterly *nugatory in practice.*

The worship of Jehovah, to be acceptable, must be a free will offering. The laws of man can reach no further, than to external deportment.

Our holy religion neither requires nor admits their aid. The heart and affections, the seat of vital religion, cannot be regulated by human legislation.

The rights of conscience are secured by universal toleration, placing all religious denominations on the footing of the most perfect equality. For the purpose of rendering this provision more certain in its operation all religious tests, as qualifications for office, are excluded. By requiring however that all officers shall be under oath, it is necessarily presupposed, that they believe in the existence and providence of God.

In times of party excitement the doctrine of libels, recognized by the common law, is sometimes employed as an engine of oppression.

The convention have endeavored to guard against the evil by making the truth of the matter published a sufficient justification in all cases, where the conduct of public men is in question, or where the public good may be promoted by a knowledge of the facts disclosed.

Pecuniary qualifications of electors have been productive of little benefit—sometimes of injustice.

They are too often relaxed or strained to suit the purposes of the day. The convention have therefore extended the right of suffrage, so that no person is disqualified for want of property, unless he be a pauper. With the same views electors under certain limitations and restrictions are also privileged from arrest on days of election.

The necessity of a reduced representation seem to be acknowledged by all. The number, to which it ought to be reduced, and the manner of making that reduction, are questions, on which scarcely two could be found to precisely agree. If some were in favor of even less than one hundred, others were the advocates of unlimited representation.

The convention adopted an intermediate course, limiting the number of representatives at not less than one hundred, nor more than two hundred, and referring the question back to the people themselves, when the number shall have reached the highest limit, whether that number shall be increased or diminished.

But the difficulties arising out of this embarrassing branch of the business entrusted to your delegates, did not here terminate. Many were advocates of a general districting system—others were equally strenuous for a representation by towns. The convention once more adopted an intermediate course.

The whole number of representatives to be elected is first to be apportioned and assigned to the several counties on the most exact principles of equity and justice. Thus the great sections of the State, the several counties, which are but larger corporations, actuated to a certain extent by a community of interests, have their due weight according to their population. The number of representatives, thus apportioned and assigned to any county, is next to be distributed among the respective towns in such county, each town, having the competent number of inhabitants, being entitled to one or more; and towns and plantations not having that number, to be classed as conveniently as possible. On any practicable system there will be fractions, and the representation of course unequal. If under the system adopted by the convention, the large towns have not their full representation, it is preserved in the county of which they are a part. They have their representatives; and even their fractions, which would otherwise be lost to them, are represented through the smaller towns of their county, who can seldom have an interest at variance with their own.

The Senate is predicated upon population.

This rule of apportionment seemed to the convention most consonant to the principles of a government by the people. Property will always possess at least its full share of influence without being specially represented in the Senate.

The Council are selected from among the people by the two branches of the Legislature. You thus avoid the idle ceremony of electing in the first instance from the Senate; and you preserve to the Senate its proper number and distinctive character. And with the view to preserve in the Council a steady regard to the public good, councilors are precluded from receiving any appointment during the time, for which they shall have been elected.

The provision respecting exempts from military duty was called for by the united voice of the militia. It tends to equalize the burthen, and to render the militia more respectable and more efficient. This duty, in its nature a personal service, ought not to fall exclusively upon any class of citizens. In the opinion of the convention, every able bodied male citizen of suitable age ought to perform it, or, in some form or other, pay an equivalent.

Free governments cannot long exist, where the people are ignorant and depraved. The due administration of our own must essentially depend upon the intelligence and virtue of our citizens. The State therefore has a deep interest in the education of our youth. Hence the convention have made it the imperative duty of the Legislature to cause schools to be supported in the several towns, and to encourage and suitably endow academies, colleges and seminaries of learning, by extending to them as far, as the circumstances of the people would authorize, the patronage of the State. At the same time it was thought proper, that the Legislature should so far retain such a general and superintending power over these institutions, as should enable it to aid the cause of good learning, and prevent the perversion or abuse of the public munificence.

To preserve the purity of the Legislature, its members under certain limitations and restrictions are disqualified, during the term, for which they are elected, from being appointed to any civil office, which may be created, or the emoluments of which may be increased, during such term. With similar views, and to prevent a system of favoritism, all persons holding lucrative appointments are excluded both from the Legislature and Council. This exclusion was deemed peculiarly proper in so far, as respects judicial officers.

Thus you preserve the several departments of the government distinct. Thus you remove those important offices as far, as possible, from all temptation to court the popular favor perhaps at the expense of justice.

On a pure, intelligent, upright, and independent judiciary, the people more immediately depend for the impartial interpretation and administration of the laws, and for protection in the enjoyment of their rights and privileges.

In the opinion of the convention, merit, not wealth, is the proper qualification for office. If with perfect safety to the people no pecuniary qualification is required for the highest offices under the United States, there is still less reason for requiring it under the government of the State. With the limitation in general, that but one important office can be held by one man, all offices are left open to all.

The settlement of our extensive vacant lands has been seriously retarded by the present unequal system of taxation. In the opinion of the convention no good reason exists, why an estate of a given value in uncultivated lands should pay only one-third so much tax, as an estate of the same value in lands under cultivation. It seemed to them not difficult to determine who best deserve the indulgence or patronage of the State, the man who brings forward and cultivates his lands, and renders them productive to the community, or the man, who suffers them to remain a useless wilderness, in order that his wealth may be increased by their rise in value, occasioned by the industry and enterprise of contiguous settlements. To remedy the evil, the convention inserted the article requiring that real estate, whether cultivated or uncultivated, shall be equally taxed according to its just value.

The apportionment of Senators and Representatives for the first Legislature, it was apprehended, might not prove perfectly equal. The convention however proceeded upon the best data in their possession, and to them it is a gratifying circumstance, that, if any injustice is done, it can be of but short duration.

An actual census of the people being about to be taken, the first Legislature will be enabled to remedy such inequalities, as shall be found to éxist, and to do exact and impartial justice to every district town and plantation.

It was not thought advisable by the convention to incumber the constitution by attempts to fix or regulate the salaries of any of your officers. This and many other objects suggested in convention are subjects of legislation and are left to the wisdom of your future legislatures.

Such, fellow citizens, are the principal provisions in the constitution submitted to you by your delegates, which embrace the material variances from the constitution, under which you have so long and so happily lived. We say principal provisions, because there are others, believed to be wholesome and salutary, which however are not deemed of sufficient importance, to be particularly noticed in this address. To the constitution itself we respectfully refer you. We solicit you once more to weigh well its provisions, to examine it as a whole. If it be not perfectly satisfactory in all its parts, judge whether, considering the differences existing in men's views and opinions, you will be likely to obtain one, more acceptable.

Your delegates have felt a deep responsibility; your approbation could not fail to be highly gratifying to them. But they wish not to bias your judgment. You act for yourselves and posterity.

In behalf and by order of the convention.

WM. P. PREBLE,
GEO. THATCHER, JR.,
BENJA. AMES,
JOSHUA GAGE,
LEONARD JARVIS,
JOHN BURGIN,
PETER C. VIRGIN,
SIMEON STETSON,
ELEAZER COBURN,
} *Committee.*

ADJOURNED SESSION.

PORTLAND,
WEDNESDAY, January 5, 1820.

This being the day to which the convention adjourned, the Honorable President and a quorum of the members of the convention assembled in the Court House in Portland, agreeably to the adjournment.

Mr. William Stevens, returned a delegate from the town of Moscow, appeared and exhibited a certificate in the usual form, of his election—which was read and thereupon

Resolved, That the said William Stevens is entitled to his seat in this convention.

Mr. Stevens accordingly took his seat.

The Hon. Mr. Parris submitted the following resolutions, which were severally read and passed:

Resolved, That the committee appointed to receive the returns from the several towns and plantations, be directed to take from the post office, such returns as have been there received since the first day of January instant.

Resolved, That —— be a committee to examine the returns of votes from the several towns and plantations, on the constitution prepared by this convention, and that the committee report the whole number given in, and what number were in favor, and what number were opposed to said constitution.

Voted, That said committee consist of nine members; and the Hon. Messrs. Parris of Portland, Thatcher of Biddeford, Cony of Augusta, Dole of Alna, Col. Pond of Bucksport, Mr. Dickinson of Machias, Mr. Stetson of Hampden, Doct. French of St. Albans, and Mr. Towle of Porter, were appointed said committee.

Resolved, That the committee on returns, report, what number of votes were legally returned, on or before the first day of

January instant, and of those so returned, the number in favor and the number opposed to the adoption of the constitution prepared by this convention.

Resolved, That —— be a committee to consider and report in what manner the adoption of the constitution, as well as our admission into the Union, if that be effected, should be announced to the people of Maine.

Voted, That said committee consist of five members, and that Col. Lewis of Gorham, Judge Ames, Mr. Campbell of Winthrop, Col. Atherton and Mr. Vance be said committee.

On motion of Judge Cony,

Resolved, That Mr. Preble of Portland, Col. Moody, Gen'l Chandler, Dr. Rose, and Mr. Johnson of Belfast, be a committee to consider and report, what business it will be proper to act upon before the convention separate.

On motion of Gen. Chandler,

Resolved, That a committee be appointed to inquire into the expediency of furnishing each town and plantation in the District of Maine, with blank forms and returns of votes for Governor, Senators and Representatives, which may be given in on the first Monday of April, 1820, and report by resolve or otherwise.

Mr. Wood of Lebanon, Mr. Allen of Norridgewock, Col. Foxcroft, Mr. Cutler of Farmington, and Dr. Snow of Atkinson, were appointed said committee.

On motion of Col. Atherton,

Resolved, That the Hon. Asa Clapp, Matthew Cobb, Isaac Ilsley, Arthur McLellan, Barrett Potter, Robert Ilsley and Levi Cutter, Esq., be a committee to provide suitable buildings and accommodations for the meeting of the Governor and Council, the Senate and House of Representatives of the State of Maine, at their first session to be holden in Portland on the last Wednesday of May, 1820.

Voted, That when the convention adjourn, it be until 10 o'clock to-morrow morning.

Adjourned accordingly.

THURSDAY, JANUARY 6, 1820.

Met according to adjournment.

Judge Parris, chairman of the committee appointed to examine the returns of votes from the several towns and plantations in Maine on the constitution prepared by this convention, having attended to the service assigned them, made the following

REPORT:

That the whole number of votes legally and seasonably returned, is nine thousand eight hundred and thirty-seven, of which nine thousand and forty are in favor of said constitution, and seven hundred and ninety-six are opposed.

And the committee further report, that the whole number of votes returned were ten thousand eight hundred and ninety-nine, of which ten thousand and twenty-five were in favor of said constitution, and eight hundred and seventy-three were opposed.

And the committee further report that the returns from the towns of Biddeford in the county of York, and Bingham in the county of Somerset, were signed by one only of the Selectmen in each town; and that the return from the town of Columbia, in the county of Washington, was not signed by the Town Clerk. And the committee do further report, that the returns from the towns of Cornish and Limington, in the county of York; Minot, in the county of Cumberland; Friendship, Hope, Cushing and Appleton plantation, in the county of Lincoln; Monroe, Eden and Trenton, in the county of Hancock; Cherryfield, in the county of Washington; Hallowell, Chesterville, Readfield, Malta and Joy, in the county of Kennebec; Turner, in the county of Oxford; New Vineyard, Fairfield, New Portland and Warsaw, in the county of Somerset; New Charleston, Foxcroft and Atkinson, in the county of Penobscot, were not returned until after the first day of January, 1820; all which is fully explained in the annexed schedule which makes a part of this report.

And the committee further report that by the return from the town of Bucksport, in the county of Hancock, although there appears to have been a meeting duly holden, and the return is duly signed and attested by the Selectmen and Town Clerk, yet it does not appear that any votes were given by the inhabitants of said town either in favor or against said constitution.

All which is submitted.

ALBION K. PARRIS, *Per Order.*

IN CONVENTION, January 6, 1820.

Read and accepted, and ordered that the report and schedule annexed, be entered upon the journals.

WILLIAM KING, *President.*

YORK COUNTY.

Towns.	Accepted.			Rejected.			Cause of Rejection.
	Whole number.	Yeas.	Nays.	Whole number.	Yeas.	Nays.	
Alfred, . .							
Arundel, . .	52	52					
Biddeford, . .	-	-	-	22	20	2	The return being signed by only one Selectman.
Berwick, . .	41	41					
Buxton, . .	124	112	12				
Cornish, . .	-	-	-	40	25	15	Not returned until after January 1, 1820.
Elliot, . . .	52	51	1				
Hollis, . . .	71	71					
Kittery, . .	31	10	21				
Lebanon, . .	109	106	3				
Limerick, . .	58	57	1				
Limington, . .	-	-	-	73	73		Not returned until after January 1, 1820.
Lyman, . . .	86	49	37				
Newfield, . .	30	17	13				
Parsonsfield, .	107	107					
Sanford, . .	95	10	85				
Saco, . . .	103	103					
Shapleigh, . .	157	25	132				
South Berwick, .	47	36	11				
Waterborough, .							
Wells, . . .	157	156	1				
York, . . .	91	91					
	1411	1094	317	135	118	17	

CUMBERLAND COUNTY.

Towns.	Accepted.			Rejected.			Cause of Rejection.
	Whole number.	Yeas.	Nays.	Whole number.	Yeas.	Nays.	
Baldwin,	30	30					
Bridgton,	78	78					
Brunswick,	90	88	2				
Cape Elizabeth,	44	44					
Danville,	44	44					
Durham,	64	58	6				
Falmouth,	58	58					
Freeport,	103	77	26				
Gorham,	95	94	1				
Gray,	87	86	1				
Harrison,	19	19					
Harpswell,	18	10	8				
Minot,	-	-	-	70	57	13	Not returned until after January 1, 1820.
North Yarmouth,	169	115	54				
New Gloucester,	119	118	1				
Otisfield,	31	26	5				
Portland,	298	286	12				
Poland,	96	94	2				
Pownal,	40	40					
Raymond,	58	52	6				
Scarborough,	69	66	3				
Standish,	68	57	11				
Westbrook,	75	74	1				
Windham,	61	61					
	1814	1675	139	70	57	13	

LINCOLN COUNTY.

Towns.	Whole number.	Yeas.	Nays.	Whole number.	Yeas.	Nays.	Cause of Rejection.
Alna,	25	18	7				
Bath,	112	111	1				
Boothbay,	38	38					
Bowdoin,	80	80					
Bowdoinham,	46	46					
Bristol,	66	64	2				
Camden,	63	59	4				
Cushing,	-	-	-	18	18		Not returned until after January 1, 1820.
Dresden,	28	28					
Edgecomb,	32	32					
Friendship,	-	-	-	22	22		Not returned until after January 1, 1820.
Georgetown,	37	36	1				
Hope,	-	-	-	52	52		Not returned until after January 1, 1820.
Jefferson,	64	52	12				
Lewiston,	67	66	1				
Lisbon,	104	103	1				
Litchfield,	86	84	2				
Montville,	53	53					
Montville Plantation,	21	20	1				
New Castle,	42	36	6				
Nobleborough,	49	49					
Palermo,	48	48					

LINCOLN COUNTY, (Continued.)

Towns.	Accepted.			Rejected.			Cause of Rejection.
	Whole number.	Yeas.	Nays.	Whole number.	Yeas.	Nays.	
Phipsburg, . .	33	33					
Putnam, . .	18	18					
St. George, . .	23	23					
Topsham, . .	61	61					
Thomaston, . .	74	74					
Union, . . .	54	49	4				
Warren, . .	42	35	7				
Waldoborough, .	35	33	2				
Whitefield, . .	42	42					
Wales, . . .	11	11					
Wiscasset, . .	57	52	5				
Woolwich, . .	39	39					
Appleton Plantation,	-	-	-	18	18		Not returned until after January 1, 1820.
	1553	1496	56	110	110		

HANCOCK COUNTY.

Towns.	Whole number.	Yeas.	Nays.	Whole number.	Yeas.	Nays.	Cause of Rejection.
Belfast, . .	71	59	12				
Belmont, . .	61	61					
Bluehill, . .	46	9	37				
Brooks, . .	24	23	1				
Brooksville, . .	18	7	11				
Bucksport, . .							
Castine, . .	33	29	4				
Deer Isle, . .	23	22	1				
Edon, . . .	-	-	-	18	18		Not returned until after January 1, 1820.
Ellsworth, . .	25	24	1				
Frankfort, . .	60	59	1				
Gouldsborough, .	14	14					
Isleborough, . .	11	10	1				
Jackson, . .	14	14					
Knox, . . .	30	30					
Lincolnville, . .	64	62	2				
Munroe, . .	-	-	-	34	33	1	Not returned until after January 1, 1820.
Mount Desert, .							
Northport, . .	13	13					
Orland, . . .	22	22					
Prospect, . .	20	20					
Penobscot, . .	32	32					
Searsmont, . .	22	22					
Swanville, . .	21	21					
Sedgwick, . .	47	23	24				
Sullivan, . .	30	29	1				
Surry, . . .	30	30					
Trenton, . .	-	-	-	22	22		Not returned until after January 1, 1820.
Thorndike, . .	21	21					
Vinalhaven, . .	32	30	2				
	784	686	98	74	73	1	

WASHINGTON COUNTY.

Towns.	Accepted.			Rejected.			Cause of Rejection.
	Whole number.	Yeas.	Nays.	Whole number.	Yeas.	Nays.	
Addison,							
Calais,	17	17					
Cherryfield,	-	-	-	14	14		Not returned until after January 1, 1820.
Columbia,	-	-	-	20	9	11	Return not signed by Town Clerk.
Dennysville,							
Eastport,	40	38	2				
Harrington,	14	12	2				
Jonesborough,	22	22					
Lubec,	44	44					
Machias,	38	38					
Orangetown,	8	8					
Perry,							
Robbinstown,	20	20					
Steuben,							
	203	199	4	34	23	11	

KENNEBEC COUNTY.

Towns.	Whole number.	Yeas.	Nays.	Whole number.	Yeas.	Nays.	Cause of Rejection.
Augusta,	81	80	1				
Belgrade,	30	28	2				
Chesterville,	-	-	-	46	38	8	Not returned until after January 1, 1820.
China,							
Clinton,	40	39	1				
Dearborn,	28	28					
Fairfax,	26	26					
Fayette,	70	66	4				
Farmington,	105	105					
Freedom,							
Gardiner,	54	54					
Greene,	70	70					
Hallowell,	-	-	-	145	142	3	Not returned until after January 1, 1820.
Harlem,	34	33	1				
Joy,	-	-	-	28	28		Not returned until after January 1, 1820.
Kingfield,	24	23	1				
Leeds,	93	93					
Malta,	-	-	-	40	40		Not returned until after January 1, 1820.
Monmouth,	98	98					
Mount Vernon,	70	70					
New Sharon,	55	53	2				
Pittstown,	28	20	8				
Readfield,	-	-	-	70	70		Not returned until after January 1, 1820.
Rome,	25	24	1				
Sidney,	74	73	1				
Temple,	24	23	1				
Unity,	44	43	1				

KENNEBEC COUNTY, (CONTINUED.)

Towns.	Accepted.			Rejected.			Cause of Rejection.
	Whole number.	Yeas.	Nays.	Whole number.	Yeas.	Nays.	
Vienna, . . .	32	32					
Vassalborough, .	50	50					
Wayne, . . .	69	68	1				
Winslow, . .	31	31					
Waterville, . .	110	110					
Wilton, . . .	62	62					
Winthrop, . .	82	64	18				
	1509	1466	43	329	318	11	

OXFORD COUNTY.

Towns.	Accepted.			Rejected.			Cause of Rejection.
	Whole number.	Yeas.	Nays.	Whole number.	Yeas.	Nays.	
Albany, . . .	21	5	16				
Bethel, . . .	85	85					
Brownfield, . .	58	57	1				
Buckfield, . .	149	146	3				
Dixfield, . .	29	27	2				
Denmark, . .							
East Andover, .	41	32	9				
Fryeburg, . .	73	73					
Gilead, . . .	23	23					
Greenwood, . .	21	21					
Hiram, . . .	29	23	1				
Hartford, . .	68	68					
Hebron, . .	78	70	8				
Jay, . . .	75	72	3				
Livermore, . .	73	71	2				
Lovel, . . .							
Mexico, . .	12	12					
Newry, . . .	34	34					
Norway, . .	77	76	1				
Paris, . . .	106	89	17				
Porter, . . .	37	36	1				
Rumford, . .	52	52					
Sweden, . .	20	20					
Sumner, . .	52	48	4				
Turner, . . .	-	-	-	88	88		Not returned until after January 1, 1820.
Waterford, . .	58	35	23				
Weld, . . .	37	37					
Woodstock, . .	29	27	2				
Plantation No. 1,	18	18					
	1350	1262	88	88	88		

SOMERSET COUNTY.

Towns.	Accepted.			Rejected.			Cause of Rejection.
	Whole number.	Yeas.	Nays.	Whole number.	Yeas.	Nays.	
Anson,	70	70					
Athens,	29	24	5				
Avon,	28	28					
Bloomfield,	52	50	2				
Bingham,	-	-	-	7	7		Return signed by only one Selectman.
Canaan,	40	40					
Corinna,	25	25					
Cornville,	27	27					
Embden,	15	14	1				
Fairfield,	-	-	-	71	67	4	Not returned until after January 1, 1820.
Freeman,	22	13	9				
Harmony,							
Industry,	29	29					
Mercer,	31	23	8				
Madison,	33	32	1				
Moscow,							
Norridgewock,	66	66					
New Portland,	-	-	-	24	9	15	Not returned until after January 1, 1820.
New Vineyard,	-	-	-	26	21	5	Not returned until after January 1, 1820.
North Hill,							
Palmyra,	27	27					
Phillips,	11	11					
Ripley,	34	34					
Starks,	39	38	1				
St. Albans,	22	22					
Solon,	33	33					
Strong,	20	20					
Warsaw,	-	-	-	19	19		Not returned until after January 1, 1820.
	653	626	27	147	123	24	

PENOBSCOT COUNTY.

Towns.	Whole number.	Yeas.	Nays.	Whole number.	Yeas.	Nays.	Cause of Rejection.
Atkinson,	-	-	-	22	22		Not returned until after January 1, 1820.
Bangor,	51	47	4				
Brewer,	42	31	11				
Carmel,	12	12					
Corinth,	18	18					
Dixmont,	28	23	5				
Dexter,	41	41					
Exeter,	27	27					
Eddington,	20	20					
Foxcroft,	-	-	-	25	25		Not returned until after January 1, 1820.

PENOBSCOT COUNTY, (CONTINUED.)

Towns.	Accepted. Whole number.	Accepted. Yeas.	Accepted. Nays.	Rejected. Whole number.	Rejected. Yeas.	Rejected. Nays.	Cause of Rejection.
Garland,	16	16					
Guilford,	27	27					
Hermon,	16	16					
Hampden,	36	36					
Levant,	6	6					
Newburg,	22	21	1				
Newport,	28	28					
New Charleston,	-	-	-	28	28		Not returned until after January 1, 1820.
Orono,	25	25					
Orrington,	58	58					
Sangerville,	17	17					
Sebec,	23	23					
Plantation No. 3, R. 6,	20	20					
Plantation No. 1, R. 3,	14	14					
Williamsburg Pl.,	13	10	3				
	560	536	24	75	75		

RECAPITULATION.

Counties.	Aggregate of votes legally returned. Whole number.	Yeas.	Nays.	Aggregate of votes not legally returned. Whole number.	Yeas.	Nays.
York,	1,411	1,094	317	135	118	17
Cumberland,	1,814	1,675	139	70	57	13
Lincoln,	1,553	1,496	56	110	110	-
Hancock,	784	686	98	74	73	1
Washington,	203	199	4	34	23	11
Kennebec,	1,509	1,466	43	329	318	11
Oxford,	1,350	1,262	88	88	88	-
Somerset,	653	626	27	147	123	24
Penobscot,	560	536	24	75	75	-
	9,837	9,040	796	1,062	985	77

IN COMMITTEE, January 6, 1820.—The foregoing is a true list of all the votes given on the adoption of the Constitution of Maine.

ALBION K. PARRIS, *Per Order.*

Attest:—ROBERT C. VOSE, *Secretary.*

Which report was read and accepted, and ordered to be entered with the special part of this report and schedule hereunto annexed, upon the journals of this convention.

Mr. Preble, chairman of the committee to whom was referred the subject of what business it will be necessary to act upon before the convention separate, having attended to the duty assigned them, made the following Report:

That in addition to the several subjects already committed to special committees, the committee submitted for the consideration of the convention, the following resolutions, which were severally read and passed:

Resolved, That the Treasurer of this convention, be and he hereby is authorized, to borrow on the credit of the State of Maine, the sum of four thousand dollars, to defray the expenditures of this convention.

Resolved, That —— be a committee to examine the books, accounts and vouchers of the Treasurer, with the view to an adjustment, and report thereon.

Gen. Wingate, Mr. Ilsley of Portland, and Mr. Gage of Augusta, were appointed on the said committee.

Resolved, That —— be a committee on the pay roll, and that they be instructed to make up the pay roll including tomorrow.

Gen. Irish, Col. Lewis, and Mr. Dearborn of Hallowell, were appointed on the said committee.

Resolved, That the Secretary of State *pro tempore,* be and he hereby is instructed to examine and ascertain what documents and papers in the office of the Secretary of the Commonwealth of Massachusetts, or elsewhere, are of importance for the use of the Legislature of Maine, and that he procure the same or authenticated copies thereof.

Resolved, That the treasurer of this convention, be directed to pay over to the Secretary of State *pro tempore,* the sum of one hundred dollars, to be accounted for by said Secretary to the Legislature of Maine.

Resolved, That this day at half-past 3 o'clock be assigned for designating by ballot, the person who, in case of the death or other disqualification of the President of this convention before the election and qualification of the Governor, under this constitution of Maine, shall have all the powers and perform all the duties which the President of this convention shall have and perform.

Resolved, That this day at half-past 3 o'clock be assigned for designating by ballot, the person who, in case of the death or other disqualification of the Secretary of State *pro tempore,* before the election and qualification of the Secretary of State, under the constitution of Maine, shall have and perform all the powers and duties of Secretary *pro tempore.*

Resolved, That this day at half-past 3 o'clock be assigned for electing by ballot, some suitable person to attend the Legislature and Executive, and address the Throne of Grace by prayer, at the organization of the government of the new State.

Gen. Wingate, was appointed on the committee on the subject of the expenses of the convention, exclusive of the pay roll, in the absence of Mr. Shepley of Saco.

Adjourned to half-past 3 o'clock this afternoon.

AFTERNOON.

Met. Agreeably to assignment, the convention proceeded to the choice of a person, who, in case of the death or other disqualification of the President of this convention, before the election and qualification of the Governor under the constitution of Maine, shall have all the powers and perform all the duties which the President of this convention shall have and perform; and Mr. Preble, Judge Thatcher, and Mr. Herrick of Bowdoinham, were appointed a committee to receive, count and sort the votes—when it appeared that the whole number of votes given were one hundred sixty-eight; necessary to a choice, eighty-five; and that the Hon. John Chandler had one hundred and ten votes, and he was declared elected. The same committee was then appointed to receive, count and sort the votes for the person who, in case of the death or other disqualification of the Secretary *pro tempore,* before the election and qualification of Secretary of State, under the constitution of Maine, shall have and perform the powers and duties of Secretary of State *pro tempore*—when it appeared that the whole number of votes given was one hundred and seventy-four; necessary to a choice, eighty-eight; and that Robert C. Vose had one hundred and seventy-two votes, and he was declared chosen.

Col. Lewis, chairman of the committee appointed to consider and report in what manner the adoption of the constitution shall be announced to the people of Maine, submitted the following resolution, which was read and accepted as amended:

Resolved, That the Secretary of this convention be directed to publish in the several newspapers printed in Maine, the certified result of the votes from the several towns and plantations in the District of Maine, upon the adoption of the constitution, as reported to the convention, and that after the fifteenth day of March next, on condition that the proposed State of Maine, shall have been admitted into the Union, the President be requested to issue his Proclamation to the people of the State of Maine, making known such admission, and that the constitution proposed by the convention and adopted by the people, is the constitution and frame of government for the State.

Mr. Wood of Lebanon, chairman of the committee on the subject of returns for Governor, Senators and Representatives, made the following Report:

No. 1, return of votes for Governor; No. 2, return of votes for Senators; No. 3, return of votes for Representatives; and that the Secretary of this convention be requested to superintend the printing and furnishing the selectmen of all the towns, and the assessors of all the plantations in the State of Maine, with a suitable number of the same—which report was read and accepted.

Agreeably to assignment, the convention proceeded to the choice of a person to attend the Legislature and Executive, and address the Throne of Grace by prayer, at the organization of the government of the new State; and the Hon. Judge Cony, Rev. Mr. Titcomb, and the Rev. Mr. Lock, of Chesterville, were appointed a committee to receive, count and sort the votes—when it appeared that the whole number of votes given were one hundred and thirty-eight; necessary to a choice, seventy; the

Rev. Mr. Nichols, of Portland, had one hundred and thirty-three votes, and he was declared chosen; and thereupon

Ordered, That the delegates from the town of Portland be requested to notify the reverend gentleman of his election.

Col. Lewis was excused from serving on the committee upon the pay roll, and Col. Atherton was appointed in his stead.

Judge Thatcher submitted the following resolution:

Resolved, That four attested copies of the constitution of the State of Maine, together with an attested copy of the report of the committee appointed to examine the returns of the votes from the several towns and plantations in Maine, on the constitution proposed to the people by this convention, be transmitted to the Supreme Executive of the Commonwealth of Massachusetts, and like copies be delivered by the Secretary of State to the Supreme Executive of the State of Maine, as soon as the government thereof shall be organized—and the same was read and committed to Mr. Moody of Hallowell, Dr. Chandler of Parris, Mr. Burr of Litchfield, Mr. Jarvis of Surry, and Major Treat, to consider and report.

Voted, That when the convention adjourn, it be until 10 o'clock to-morrow morning.

Adjourned accordingly.

FRIDAY, January 7, 1820.

Met according to adjournment.

Gen. Wingate, chairman of the committee appointed to examine the books, accounts and vouchers of the Treasurer, submitted the following Report: That it appears by the accounts presented to the committee by the Hon. Albion K. Parris, Treasurer of this convention, accompanying this report, he has received the sum of nineteen thousand seven hundred forty-two dollars and twelve cents, that he has paid to the members of this convention for their travel and attendance the first session, the sum of sixteen thousand dollars, and for accounts allowed, interest and incidental expenses at the first session, seven hundred eighty-two dollars and twenty-nine cents, leaving a balance in the hands of the Treasurer of two thousand nine hundred fifty-nine dollars and eighty-three cents, to be applied in part payment of the expenses of the present session of the convention. The pay roll of the present session not having been placed in the hands of the Treasurer, the committee have not been enabled to adjust the accounts of the expenditures of the present session, and therefore recommend the passage of the following resolves, which are respectfully submitted:

Resolved, That the Treasurer of this convention be directed to account with the first Legislature of Maine, for the balance of money remaining in his hands, after defraying the appropriations made by this convention.

Resolved, That the Treasurer be allowed as compensation for his services, the one-half of one per centum on all moneys paid out by him, under the direction of this convention—which report and resolutions were severally read and accepted.

The return of votes from the town of Steuben upon the question of the constitution was this day received by the Hon. President, and by him communicated to the convention, whereby it appeared that the inhabitants of said town gave in seventeen votes in favor of the constitution and none against it.

Ordered, That said return be placed on file.

Gen. Irish, chairman of the committee upon the pay roll, made a report, by which it appeared that the amount of travel and attendance, due the several members the present session, amounting in the whole to the sum of four thousand two hundred and sixteen dollars; which was read, and

Ordered, That the Treasurer of this convention be authorized to pay the several persons borne on the pay roll, the sum set against their names respectively.

Hon. Mr. Gage, chairman of the committee on accounts, made a report that the sums set against the names of the following persons, to wit: to

Francis Douglass, for printing,	$178 20
Christopher Rand, for sundry expenses,	42 26
Aaron Chamberlain,	15 25
Robert C. Vose, Secretary, for services and expenses,	118 20
William B. Peters, Sergeant-at-Arms,	6 00
Thomas Bailey,	6 00
N. G. Jewett, a Clerk in the lobbies,	6 00
Robert Ilsley, Post Master,	11 39½
	$383 30½

Which report was read, and

Ordered, That the Treasurer pay the several persons borne on this roll, the sums set against their names respectively, in full for their services.

Mr. Moody of Hallowell, chairman of the committee to whom was referred the resolutions submitted yesterday by the Hon. Judge Thatcher, reported the following resolution as taken into a new draft:

Resolved, That the President of this convention, cause to be transmitted to the Supreme Executive of the Commonwealth of Massachusetts, one attested manuscript copy of the constitution of the State of Maine, and the reports of the committee appointed to examine the return of the votes of the several towns and plantations, upon the question of the adoption of the constitution, and also an attested manuscript copy of the proceedings of this convention—which resolution was read and accepted.

The Hon. Judge Thatcher, read in his place the following resolution:

Resolved, unanimously, That the thanks of this convention be presented to the Honorable William King, for the dignified and impartial manner with which he has discharged the duties of the chair, during our deliberations—which resolution was again read by the Secretary and unanimously adopted.

The Honorable President then made the following reply:

Gentlemen of the Convention:—For the sentiments which you have expressed, I feel particularly grateful;—they come, I perceive, from an old and respected friend, from whom political considerations have perhaps too long separated me. My friend, on this occasion, does not remember them—they are, therefore, erased from my recollection forever.

The constitution, gentlemen, which you have presented with so much unanimity to our fellow-citizens, an unexampled majority have adopted. Your business has therefore now terminated; to the public it has been most useful; to yourselves most honorable, being now enrolled as the fathers of the constitution.

Permit me, gentlemen, to hope that the constitution with which God has been pleased, through you, to bless us, may long preserve the liberties, and promote the happiness of all our fellow-citizens; and that for your services, you may not only receive the respect of the virtuous of your own time, but the regard of posterity.

The business of the convention being completed, on motion of the Hon. Judge Cony,

Voted, That the convention adjourn without day.

Adjourned accordingly.

ATTEST:—R. C. VOSE, *Secretary.*

STATE OF MAINE.

Resolves to authorize the printing of the Journal of the Constitutional Convention.

Resolved, That the secretary of state be directed to cause one thousand copies to be printed, of the journal of the convention which framed the constitution of Maine.

Resolved, That copies of the same be transmitted to such persons and corporations as are entitled under existing resolves to receive copies of the laws of the state, and that the remainder be retained for the future disposition of the legislature.

[Approved April 10, 1856.]

www.ingramcontent.com/pod-product-compliance
Lightning Source LLC
LaVergne TN
LVHW021427110826
845150LV00007B/2116

* 9 7 8 1 4 2 5 5 0 7 4 8 0 *